# ETHICS AND VALUES IN APPLIED SOCIAL RESEARCH

## Allan J. Kimmel

**Applied Social Research Methods Series**
**Volume 12**

**SAGE** PUBLICATIONS
*The International Professional Publishers*
Newbury Park   London   New Delhi

*For information address:*

SAGE Publications, Inc.
2111 West Hillcrest Drive
Newbury Park, California 91320

SAGE Publications Ltd.
28 Banner Street
London EC1Y 8QE
England

SAGE Publications India Pvt. Ltd.
M-32 Market
Greater Kailash I
New Delhi 110 048 India

Printed in the United States of America

Library of Congress Cataloging-in-Publication Data

Kimmel, Allan J.
    Ethics and values in applied social research / Allan J. Kimmel.
        p.   cm. — (Applied social research methods series; v. 12)
    Bibliography: p.
    Includes indexes.
    ISBN 0-8039-2631-6   ISBN 0-8039-2632-4 (pbk.)
    1. Social sciences—Research—Moral and ethical aspects.
I. Title.  II. Series.
H62.K495   1988          87-25166
300'.72—dc19

THIRD PRINTING, 1990

# ETHICS
# AND VALUES
# IN APPLIED
# SOCIAL
# RESEARCH

**Applied Social Research Methods Series**
**Volume 12**

# APPLIED SOCIAL RESEARCH
# METHODS SERIES

*Series Editor:*
**LEONARD BICKMAN, Peabody College, Vanderbilt University, Nashville**
*Series Associate Editor:*
**DEBRA J. ROG, Vanderbilt University, Washington, DC**

# CONTENTS

# PREFACE

My first introduction to research ethics came when I was a student enrolled in an undergraduate experimental social psychology course at the University of Maryland. The American Psychological Association had just approved its current ethical guidelines for human subject research. We discussed those guidelines and their implications in class, but only after I had already begun work with a fellow student on an original experiment for which we would be graded. Consistent with most social psychological research at that time, our study was conducted in the laboratory and it involved an elaborate deception. Our newly acquired insights into the ethical imperatives of laboratory research, however, quickly caused us concern about our use of deception. We realized that it was too late in the course to redesign our experiment so that our subjects would not have to be deceived; instead, we resolved to take the subject debriefing that followed the collection of data a lot more seriously than we had done previously. Although I have never felt entirely comfortable with our decision to continue deceiving the very persons we relied on to donate their valuable time as participants in our study, I realize, in retrospect, that our pragmatic decision probably was not an atypical compromise.

This book is intended to provide a discussion of and insights into ethical problems and dilemmas faced by social scientists engaged in applied social research. It was written in large part so that social researchers will be better able to anticipate ethical problems in their applied studies *before* they occur, in order to avoid them entirely or else become more skillful in coping with them. All too often, it seems, researchers do not fully appreciate the complexities of ethical issues and dilemmas until they are caught up in them while in the midst of conducting research. By that time, it is likely to be too late to cope effectively with the problems in a reasoned and objective manner, and less than satisfactory compromises between ethical and methodological considerations are likely to result.

The book is intended primarily for advanced undergraduates, graduate students, and researchers in the social and behavioral sciences. It includes case studies and offers suggestions for resolving ethical conflicts and developing research alternatives. Throughout the book, the potential conflicts between ethical and professional values are addressed so as to assess the ethical objections that have been leveled against applied social research tactics and goals. It is hoped that this discussion will contribute to a fuller understanding of the methods of social research and the organization of scientific activity.

There are a number of people to thank for their assistance during the preparation of this volume. I am especially grateful to Debra Rog and Leonard Bickman, editors of the series, for giving me the opportunity to write it. They, as well as two reviewers, Thomas Murray and Greg Andranovich, commented on an earlier draft and offered a number of useful suggestions that I have tried to incorporate in the chapters that follow. I believe their suggestions have made for a fuller and richer book. Donald Campbell furnished helpful background materials, including some of the working papers he prepared for the National Commission for the Protection of Human Subjects of Biomedical and Behavioral Research. He also provided a number of enviable insights into the subtle ethical problems likely to be encountered in the conduct of preventive intervention research. Finally, I am particularly indebted to Ralph Rosnow, who served not unlike a "silent partner" in this enterprise. His many comments and repeated feedback on earlier drafts of the chapters were invaluable and he is in large part responsible for inspiring me to write the book.

Allan J. Kimmel
Fitchburg, Massachusetts

# 1

# *Introduction*

Since World War II, ethical issues in the social sciences have become a topic of growing concern as researchers try to ensure that their studies are directed toward worthwhile goals and that the welfare of their subjects and their research colleagues is protected. In recent decades, scientific and societal mechanisms and collective guidelines have evolved to provide assurance both to investigators within social science disciplines (anthropology, political science, psychology, and sociology) and to the general public that the resolution of research dilemmas will be morally acceptable. But ethical decision making depends largely on the individual researcher's awareness and interpretation of these mechanisms and guidelines and, in many cases, the issues lack the clarity required for resolution.

The ethical issues encountered in applied social research are subtle and complex, raising difficult moral dilemmas that, at least on a superficial level, appear unresolvable. These dilemmas often require the researcher to strike a delicate balance between the scientific requirements of methodology and the human rights and values potentially threatened by the research. As such, the underlying guiding research principle is to proceed both ethically and without threatening the validity of the research endeavor insofar as possible. It thus is essential that investigators continually ask how they can conduct themselves ethically and still make progress through sound and generalizable research. In subsequent chapters, current ethical standards and regulations will be reviewed, and their implications as guiding mechanisms will be discussed in the context of dilemmas encountered in actual research cases.

The intent in this first chapter is to highlight the importance of questions of ethics and values in social research. Toward that end, the goals of applied social research are described and contrasted with those of basic research endeavors, and some illustrative case studies of ethically controversial investigations in the research literature are reviewed to sensitize the reader to the importance of ethical considerations at all stages of the research process.

## THE GOALS OF BASIC
## AND APPLIED SCIENCE

While sharing certain fundamental principles of research, social scientists may choose to direct their scientific activity from a "pure" or "applied" orientation. The basic distinction—albeit an oversimplified one—underlying this dichotomy is that "pure" science remains unchallenged by practical, concrete social problems and issues while "applied" research is essentially atheoretical in nature (Pepitone, 1981). Individuals who limit their scientific activity to purely theoretical work unrelated in any apparent way to real-world problems are typically referred to as "basic" researchers. Basic researchers hold that the proper course of science is the objective study and ultimate solution of basic scientific questions, regardless of whether their solutions have practical applications.

Around the turn of the twentieth century, social science research first became largely guided by a mechanistic paradigm or conceptual scheme borrowed—not by accident—from the experimental approach of the natural sciences. Since that time, basic researchers typically have viewed themselves as value-free "technicians," maintaining an active role in the discovery of truth but a passive role in determining the societal use of their findings (Rosnow, 1981). The assumption underlying this position of scientific nonresponsibility was (and still is, to a large extent) that although research findings can be used for good or bad ends, knowledge is ethically neutral. Working from this value-free tradition, basic researchers generally agree that their work is objective and morally neutral (as implied by the labels "pure" and "basic"), since their goal is the disinterested and impersonal pursuit of scientific knowledge for its own sake.

Some critics of the basic science tradition maintain that pure research is not value free since, in their view, it is immoral *not* to use the knowledge we have from theoretical research to attempt to reduce real-life social problems (e.g., Baumrin, 1970; Weber, 1949). But other critics of the supposed moral neutrality of basic science (e.g., Giddens, 1976, 1979; Smith, 1978) have argued the reverse point by claiming that, in fact, there *have* been past abuses in applications of "pure knowledge" (such as splitting the atom and Hiroshima, in vitro fertilization and test tube babies, and the like). Further, critics contend that basic research often entails the use of unethical procedures for obtaining knowledge (as when human subjects are harmed during a theoretical study), and they point out the potential destructiveness of some knowledge for personal and social life, such as the undermining of character and social customs (Luria, 1976; Smith, 1978). Thus when one considers the basic scientist's "right to know" within a larger social perspective, it is apparent that such a right—which is an implicit assumption within the pure science framework—can conflict with the obligation to do no harm (Steininger, Newell, & Garcia, 1984).

Perhaps in reaction to the apparent constraints and limited utility of a purely theoretical approach, some social scientists have made serious attempts to introduce and firmly establish social relevance into their work. In psychology, for example, a shift away from a purely theoretical approach has occurred at various stages in the development of the profession. Until World War I, psychology avoided any shift toward application in order to maintain its stature as a pure and objective science. Any tendency toward application was criticized adamantly by the more traditional basic researchers, such as E. B. Titchener, a staunch experimentalist. Titchener vigorously criticized the establishment of the behaviorism school during the 1920s for asking psychologists to trade a science for a technology that was not firmly rooted in theory (O'Donnell, 1979). Years later, William McGuire (1965, p. 139), another leading experimentalist, proclaimed that a research approach that emphasized application rather than theory was one "as inelegant and inefficient as trying to push a piece of cooked spaghetti across the table from the back end." Since World War I, apparently in reaction to social and professional forces, the pendulum has at times swung away from pure research and toward application as opportunities emerged for an action-oriented science in psychology. However, each attempt at relevance brought with it a set of subtle, complex ethical issues that seriously threatened the ideals of scientific objectivity and moral neutrality (Rosnow, 1981).

It may be that in their impatience to find relevance in their work psychologists failed to consider the ethical implications of using many of their established laboratory procedures in applied settings. Argyris (1975) has suggested, for example, that because so much scientific social psychology has been based on the manipulation and control of variables in laboratory experiments, psychologists who attempt to solve social problems do so by trying to manipulate and control variables in the natural world, perhaps inappropriately. If this assessment is valid, it is not difficult to understand why many of the ethical dilemmas encountered in theoretical laboratory research (such as those involving informed consent, debriefing, and confidentiality) have appeared in applied settings as well. Only recently have psychologists begun to consider alternative strategies for conducting research and for producing social change, such as enlisting individuals as collaborators, rather than "subjects." Advocates of this so-called "role play" approach maintain that the enterprise of collecting data or producing change can thus better serve the mutual interests of both psychologist and coworker participant.

Other social science disciplines, such as political science, have undergone similar shifts in orientation during their development. In political science, a focus on methodology and objective inquiry gradually gave way during the 1940s to an emphasis on problems that arise in the adjustment of individuals to their society. This policy-science approach stressed that the political scientist should choose problems for study that have a bearing on the major policy issues of the time, and that are consistent with his or her values and the goals and objectives of democratic society (Lasswell, 1951). See Lerner and Lasswell (1951) and Rein (1976) for in-depth considerations of the policy approach in political science.

Many individuals within the scientific community would argue that research ethics become increasingly important as the results of investigations acquire policy, professional, and personal implications outside the social science professions. However, this is not meant to imply that one can avoid responsibility for knowledge produced by restricting his or her scientific activity to a basic science approach. Conversely, the view that only applied research is ethical because of its assumed potential for social benefits is a short-sighted one, since some of the greatest breakthroughs in science have come about through basic theoretical research. For example, chemistry did not advance as a science until chemists shifted away from an applied end (the creation of gold) to a concern for understanding chemistry at a theoretical level (Diener & Crandall, 1978).

When the dichotomy between pure and applied science is more closely evaluated, moral distinctions tend to blur. There are those who currently maintain that the "pure" versus "applied" distinction is a misconception and should be rejected (Georgoudi & Rosnow, 1985; Pepitone, 1981). According to this argument, because applied research often leads to theoretical understanding, and theoretical advances permit practical applications, the two types of research may not be as different as they initially appear. Theory does not arise in a social vacuum apart from concrete events that gave impetus to it (Sarason,

1981), and, conversely, theories of social behavior must withstand tests of practical application within concrete social settings in order to become established within the scientific community (Georgoudi & Rosnow, 1985). Consistent with this view, social psychologist Kurt Lewin (1947) advanced the idea that theoretical advances and the understanding of social problems are interdependent. Lewin proposed an "action research" that centered on studying things by changing them and observing the effects of the change. In Lewin's view, it is possible to be a scientific researcher who is, at the same time, concerned with the potential application of one's findings. Social scientists can hardly be expected to obtain a complete understanding of such social phenomena as leadership, political and economic behavior, and interpersonal relations without the observation of individuals within their sociocultural context (Pepitone, 1981).

It is possible that even the most scientific social researchers have been engaging in action-oriented research, albeit with a theoretical orientation. Scientific training inculcates an advocacy of rigid objectivity while pressing for theoretical expression. The irony of the situation is that adherence to a theory can cause the scientist to select problems, ask questions, devise experiments, and obtain answers that are objective only with regard to a particular theory. When one views the history of science, it is apparent that strict scientific objectivity is honored in the breach as much as in the observation (Lamberth & Kimmel, 1981).

## PREVENTIVE INTERVENTION: AN ILLUSTRATIVE EXAMPLE OF APPLIED SOCIAL RESEARCH

The primary goal of an "action-oriented" science is to accumulate facts and principles for immediate application to social problems and for the betterment of the human condition. Applied social researchers conduct their studies in the hope that they yield results that have significant potential value in the formulation or improvement of programs intended to help solve a wide range of social problems (Rivlin & Timpane, 1975).

Social scientists who apply their science in real-life settings where people live and work, are inevitably acting on morally relevant decisions about what should be changed and why (Reynolds, 1979). Values enter into applied social investigations at various levels of the research process: with the decision that there is a problem, definition of the problem in terms of its presumed cause and potential solutions, and identification and selection of individuals for research participation and targeted change (Fischer, 1980; Warwick & Kelman, 1973).

Recent research developments in the area of preventive intervention research provide a useful illustration of the nature and goals of a typical applied social research endeavor, and suggest how values are inseparable from that endeavor. As a form of social intervention, prevention research involves the experimental or quasi-experimental investigation of natural behavior in community settings. Many of the areas of application of prevention investigations have involved strictly controlled treatments for low-income, minority populations. Typically, these treatments are educational in nature, oriented toward teaching people different ways to think, behave, and interact in order to protect them from potential depression (e.g., Muñoz, Glish, Soo-Hoo, & Robertson, 1982), difficulties in interpersonal interactions (e.g., Spivack, Platt, & Shure, 1976; Spivack & Shure, 1974), drug abuse (e.g., Polich, Ellickson, Reuter, & Kahan, 1984), and the like. Many of the preventive intervention studies now being undertaken at regional, federally funded preventive intervention research centers (PIRCs) involve random assignment of treatment and no-treatment (or other contrast) conditions to experimental and control participants, and in that sense are "true" rather than "quasi" social experiments.

As with other forms of applied social research methods, there are a number of general ethical requirements for preventive research techniques. These include a rational basis and need for the proposed study, proper study design, competent and qualified investigators and supporting staff, suitable research environments, adequate equipment and materials, and appropriate selection, number, and type of research participants or subject groups. Compensatory measures, including health and medical care, and economic, social, and other types of reparation also must be available to those who may be harmed as a result of the research.

Unlike many theoretical investigations in controlled settings and natural contexts, but more typical of applied research in general, prevention studies often deal with significant aspects of social, psychological, behavioral, and economic functioning, and require considerable resources and staff to be conducted adequately. In this context, the protection of subjects' rights to privacy, confidentiality, and informed consent perhaps represents the primary responsibility of the research team in maintaining respect for individual research participants. No less important, however, are the subtler ethical issues associated with the methodological requirements of random selection and assignment of participants to experimental conditions. Ethical questions likely to be encountered in this regard involve the use of volunteer subject groups, and the appropriateness of including untreated control groups in social intervention studies. In addition to these ethical issues, perhaps the most serious to be considered involves the unintended adverse effects of an intervention effort. There are several examples of unanticipated consequences (see, for example, description of the Cambridge-Somerville Youth Study below), and these serve as stark reminders of the potentially damaging effects of applied research in general.

Values play an important role in prevention intervention studies because the research represents an attempt to prevent mental health patterns the scientist believes are potentially damaging to others. The role of values underlying ethical decision making in applied social research will be more fully considered in Chapter 7; however, a central theme running throughout the book is that discussions, debates, and arguments relevant to ethical concerns require a consideration of a number of scientific and moral points of view. Research suggests that answers to ethical questions may depend as much on one's view of science and one's general ethical philosophy as they depend on the current state of scientific research (e.g., Schlenker & Forsyth, 1977).

## CASE STUDIES IN
## SOCIAL RESEARCH ETHICS

It is clear in the discussion of preventive intervention research above that ethical responsibility is essential at all stages of the research process, from design of a study—including how subjects are recruited and how they are treated during the course of these procedures—to the consequences of their participation after having revealed certain information and having in some sense increased their own vulnerability, or the vulnerability of others in the community (Kelman, 1972). What follows below are four brief case studies that serve to illustrate unanticipated ethical dilemmas that might emerge during the social research process: (1) Project Camelot, a political science research project that focused on the determinants of revolution in Latin American nations and that was quickly condemned as a counterinsurgency effort; (2) the Cambridge-Somerville Youth Study, a secondary prevention program aimed at delinquent youths, in which all reasonable steps were taken to protect research participants, but that nevertheless resulted in unanticipated negative consequences; (3) the "Springdale" study, a sociological investigation of a small town in upstate New York, which demonstrates how serious infractions of the right to privacy can arise from the publication of research findings that fail to disguise the identities of individual participants; and (4) the "tearoom trade" study of homosexual behavior in public restrooms, which raised questions about the extent to which disguised research practices can be used to study the ongoing behavior of unsuspecting participants.

*Project Camelot.* The results of social research are often perceived to be useful to those who seek either to justify change or to retard it. As a result, powerful control elements of society, such as the administrative sector of the social system that supports these research efforts, recognize the potential usefulness of research concerning social structure and change. Project Camelot is considered by many social scientists to be a clear example of a project that could have generated knowledge that, in the wrong hands, might have provided a potential for dramatic misuse (Levin, 1981; Reynolds, 1979). Sponsored by the U.S. Department of Defense, the $6 million project focused on the determinants of revolution in various Latin American countries.

The impetus for Project Camelot came from the office of the Army's Chief of Research and Development, and the project subsequently was carried out by the Special Operations Research Office of the American University, Washington, D.C., which was under contract with the Army to conduct "research in the social and behavior science fields in support of the Army's mission" (in *Behavioral Sciences and the National Security*, 1965, p. 192). Project Camelot was described in an Army fact sheet as a "social science project on preconditions of internal conflict, and on effects of indigenous governmental actions—easing, exacerbating or resolving—on these preconditions" (statement by Senator J. W. Fulbright on Department of Defense Research in Foreign Policy Matters, *Congressional Record*, August 25, 1965, p. 20906). The objectives of the investigation, according to Irving Louis Horowitz's (1967, p. vi) detailed account of the project, were "to devise procedures for assessing the potential for internal war within national societies" and "to identify with increased degrees of confidence those actions which a government might take to relieve conditions which are assessed as giving rise to potential for internal war." If successful, the project would have resulted in a systematic description of the events that preceded, occurred during, and followed either a peaceful or violent change in government.

In essence, Project Camelot was predicated on the assumption that with increased knowledge of the problem of counterinsurgency, the Army could effectively cope with the problem when it developed in other nations. The project was officially initiated in December 1964 (shortly after the United States had sent Marines to the Dominican Republic) when a project director was appointed and a number of social scientists (including sociologists, political scientists, economists, and a psychologist) were recruited to serve as consultants. The consultants were to provide technical support, mostly on a temporary basis, or to maintain longer-term responsibility for aspects of the research design. The actual investigation was to involve surveys and other field studies in various Latin American countries, and ultimately elsewhere in the world.

Project Camelot was very quickly condemned by social scientists who viewed it as an attempt by the Department of Defense to intervene in the internal affairs of Latin American countries by sponsoring research designed to reduce the likelihood of revolution. Under pressure from several fronts, Secretary of Defense Robert McNamara canceled the study on June 8, 1965, prior to initiation of the actual fieldwork within the targeted countries. The demise of Project Camelot has been traced to adverse reaction that arose in Chile, following certain informal efforts to establish working relations with Chilean social scientists (Horowitz, 1967). The project was brought to the attention of Chilean intellectuals and, subsequently, to certain members of the Chilean Senate and various left-wing elements in that country, who reacted with a number of charges against the U.S. government and its researchers. The controversy eventually led to a presidential communication instructing the U.S. State Department to review all federally funded investigations involving cross-societal research activities potentially affecting foreign policy.

The controversy surrounding Project Camelot demonstrates the drawbacks of social research conducted under the sponsorship of organizations, such as the Army, whose primary function is that of control. It is difficult to say whether the project would have met with similar attacks had it been carried out by social researchers with a sufficient degree of autonomy from the government. Due to the source of financial support, there was considerable suspicion that the knowledge developed from the investigation would be used to help prevent changes in existing governments, and though the actual objectives and intended use of findings were never publicly specified, the suspicions and ensuing political controversy created enough international hostility to cause termination of the project (Beals, 1969; Reynolds, 1979). Outside social science circles, Project Camelot had the overall effect of calling into question the legitimacy of social science research in general, including several other research projects in South America that were stopped as a result (Glazer, 1972).

The debate over the appropriateness of Project Camelot raged on for several years after its termination, and the political and ethical reactions to the study reflect the vastly different views that social scientists hold about such issues (Sjoberg, 1967). Whereas some social scientists accepted the objectives of the American government and the military as legitimate, others clearly challenged the goals of the project's sponsors and their failure to consider the positive aspects of revolution. For example, Glazer (1972, p. 39) explained his condemnation of the project on three counts: "for simply assuming that the U.S. military has a legitimate role in dealing with social problems of other countries, for asserting that this country's foreign policy was a major factor in determining the site of research, and for implying that internal war is always the greatest threat to a population's well-being."

The major ethical problem encountered in Project Camelot (and many other similar investigations) was the inability of the researchers to acquire knowledge while achieving a sufficient amount of autonomy from controlling governmental units. According to Sjoberg (1967), this type of problem intensifies as the social sciences play an increasingly larger role in governmental and other large-scale organization activities. Since Project Camelot, other similar cases have come to light (such as those involving the CIA's sponsorship of research), revealing that the project was not an isolated case. As social scientists attempt to orient their research in the direction of broader human concerns while accepting support from specific social organizations, major ethical and political dilemmas, such as those characterized by Project Camelot, will continue to arise.

*The Cambridge-Somerville Youth Study.* The Cambridge-Somerville Youth Study serves as a strong reminder of the need to conduct evaluated pilot studies in order to assess the potentially damaging effects of treatments, and to take precautionary measures to guard against them. In 1939, Richard Clark Cabot, a social philosopher and physician, began an experimental childhood treatment program intended to prevent delinquency among boys (aged 5 to 13) in Boston. The subsequent research program became known as the Cambridge-Somerville Youth Study (Powers & Witmer, 1951), and is notable because of its truly experimental nature and the random assignment of more than 500 research participants. Although methodologically the Cambridge-Sommerville stands as an exemplary example of a large-scale, long-term social experiment, it apparently is one in which the treatment under study unexpectedly hurt more than it helped.

Cabot's research involved 506 boys, half of whom were judged as "difficult" or delinquency prone, while the remainder were judged as "average." An equal number of individuals from each group were randomly assigned to a preventively oriented counseling program during which they received tutoring, medical assistance, and friendly advice for approximately five years. The other subjects were randomly assigned to a no-treatment control group.

More than thirty years later, in 1975 and 1976, Joan McCord and her research team conducted an evaluation of the Cambridge-Somerville Study in an attempt to assess its long-term effects. Through the use of official records and personal contacts, McCord (1978) obtained information about the early study's long-term effects on the life experiences of 95% of the original participants. The evaluation compared men who had been in the treatment group with "matched mates" from the control group. Although subjective judgments of the program's value by those who received its services were found by McCord to be generally favorable, the objective criteria presented a quite different and disturbing picture. None of the comparisons between the treatment and control groups showed that the prevention program had improved the lives of those in the treatment group; in fact, the only significant differences favored those who had *not* experienced the intervention. Treated subjects were more likely than controls to evidence signs of alcoholism and serious mental illness, died at a younger age, suffered from more stress-related diseases, tended to be employed in lower-prestige occupations, and were more likely to commit second crimes.

As a plausible interpretation of the unintended effects of the Cambridge-Somerville Project, McCord suggested that a dependency upon agency assistance might have developed among treated subjects, and that these individuals then experienced resentment when the outside assistance was no longer available. McCord also conjectured that the treatment program may have created in treated subjects high expectations that led to feelings of deprivation in subsequent experiences, or perhaps increased the likelihood that they misperceived themselves as in need of help in order to justify receiving the program's services.

Whatever the explanation for the study's outcome, McCord's follow-up revealed not only that the Cambridge-Somerville Project apparently failed to achieve one of its basic goals in preventing treated subjects from committing crimes, but also seems to have produced negative side effects no doubt unanticipated by Cabot and members of the research team who implemented the program. Equally distressing is that such findings in social research are hardly unique. Other prevention programs that increased dysfunctional risk have been reported by Fo and O'Donnell (1975) and Gersten, Langner, and Simcha-Fagan (1979). Lorion (1984) has pointed to the effects of widespread adoption of open classrooms for learning disabled children, and swine flue vaccinations for the elderly, as representative additional examples of the unintended consequences of social intervention strategies. It should be noted, however, that when a widely accepted, ongoing intervention produces the negative effects and evaluation research uncovers these effects, the research may be viewed as having served as a positive moral force. In such cases, the research will have uncovered the negative effects of a treatment that was both common and thought to be positive.

*The "Springdale" Case.* Whereas ethics in social research frequently involves the deliberate attempt to affect phenomena through direct manipulations, a substantial amount of research in the social sciences instead focuses on descriptions of natural processes. Social science research at the descriptive level is characterized by procedures that emphasize the direct observation of specific individuals or a social system, and the intensive review of natural behaviors and events. Such an approach is commonly employed by anthropologists, sociologists, and psychologists who are allowed access to a social setting and an opportunity to talk to participants in an attempt to discover and describe important social processes and cultural structures of a group. These investigations are often undertaken with the full knowledge of the individuals involved, and, unlike experimental and other types of research, the investigations are more likely to be merely exploratory, resulting in descriptions that tend to be discursive and anecdotal (Reynolds, 1979).

Serious infractions of the right to privacy and anonymity can arise from the publication of research findings that expose community institutions or unique individuals to public scrutiny. As a consequence, the ethical issues associated with descriptive field studies of social structure, group or community activity, and the like, tend to arise in the reporting or publishing phase rather than during the data-collection stage, as is more typical of experimental investigations (Levin, 1981).

The descriptive field study of a small town in upstate New York (Vidich & Bensman, 1958) clearly illustrates how the impact of indirect effects occurring after the research is completed may be substantially greater than that of direct effects that occur during data collection. In their book *Small Town in Mass Society: Class, Power and Religion in a Rural Community*, Vidich and Bensman describe the political and social life of a community identified by the fictitious name "Springdale," based on Vidich's observations while living there for two and one-half years. The book was intended to "explore the foundations of social life in a community which lacks the power to control the institutions that regulate and determine its existence" (Vidich & Bensman, 1958, p. vii).

Before the Springdale project was begun, the town's residents were assured by the research staff that no individuals would be identified in printed reports, and, in fact, a code of ethics was specifically devised for the project. The stated purpose of the code was to safeguard "the integrity and welfare of research participants" through the protection of their privacy and anonymity, and by assuring that the data collected would remain confidential (Bell & Bronfenbrenner, 1959). However, when a manuscript of Vidich and Bensman's book was reviewed prior to its publication there was some concern that, while individuals within the book were given fictitious names, certain persons were identifiable within Springdale and described in ways that would be damaging to them (Johnson, 1982). This assessment turned out to be all too prophetic. Publication of the study embarrassed members of the town, who recognized and strongly objected to the descriptions of various members of their community, including its leaders, despite the attempt to disguise their identities.

Springdale residents no doubt felt that the researchers' promise of anonymity had been betrayed. The tone of the book, which has been characterized as condescending and patronizing, also came into question, as did the causal attribution of attitudes and motives to the various members of the community (Reynolds, 1979). For example, one passage in the book reads as follows:

> The people of Springdale are unwilling to recognize the defeat of their values, their personal impotence in the face of larger events, and many failures in their ways of life. By techniques of self-avoidance and self-deception, they strive to avoid facing issues that, if recognized, would threaten the total fabric of their personal and social existence. Instead of facing the issues, they make compromises and modify their behavior in some cases, and reaffirm their traditional patterns in other cases. (p. 314)

The citizens of Springdale reacted to publication of the book by publicly lampooning the researchers in a Fourth of July parade, and by refusing further cooperation with any social scientists whatsoever, thereby negating the possibility of replication and long-term follow-up.

The ethical question raised by the Springdale affair, and one often associated with the publication of fieldwork, is "To what extent is the author of a community study obligated to pursue the anonymity of the people of the community studied?" (Johnson, 1982). When research participants can recognize themselves in embarrassing or uncomplimentary descriptions in print, resulting negative effects might include a reduction in their self-esteem and loss of confidence in the scientific process. At the same time, their claim that the portrayal of their social structure is misleading calls into question the accuracy of the report, and inevitably reduces confidence in the descriptions contained within it. Ironically, their antagonism to social research, resulting from their earlier experience, precludes any follow-up study to resolve the problem of accuracy.

*The "Tearoom Trade" Study.* Many ethical issues involved in the conduct of social research concern the use of deception, whether it is employed in experimental studies in which a treatment is administered to a group of unsuspecting subjects, or in less controlled research where respondents are secretly observed or asked disguised questions. While the use of deception in social research poses a number of ethical issues, perhaps the most serious consequence is that certain forms of deception often invade the privacy of research participants by violating their right to choose the circumstances and extent to which their opinions, beliefs, and behaviors are revealed or withheld from others (Ruebhausen & Brim, 1966). The violation of subjects' right to privacy is a likely outcome of participant observation research in which an investigator assumes a disguised role.

The case of sociologist Laud Humphreys's "tearoom trade" study perhaps best illustrates the ethical problems that can emerge in disguised research in public settings. As a doctoral candidate in sociology at Washington University, Humphreys became a participant-observer in a number of homosexual acts occurring in "tearooms"—public restrooms where homosexuals engaged in sexual activity. He assumed the role of tearoom "watchqueen" by serving as a lookout with the responsibility to warn of approaching strangers in exchange for the right to observe the homosexual activity.

Humphreys sought to learn about the lifestyles and motives of the men who congregated in the tearooms, but who otherwise seemed to lead normal heterosexual lives as accepted members of their communities. By obtaining the confidence of some of the men he observed, Humphreys revealed to them his role as a scientist and was able to convince them to talk openly about their lives. Upon learning that these men were among the better educated of the tearoom participants, Humphreys sought to obtain a more representative sample by tracing the registration numbers of subjects' automobiles to determine their home addresses. A year later, Humphreys altered his appearance and, claiming to be a health service interviewer, questioned his subjects at home.

The findings of Humphreys's research revealed that only a small percentage of his subjects were members of the gay community. Many of the subjects studied were married men who did not think of themselves as either homosexual or bisexual, but whose marriages were marked with tension. As might be expected, publication of the tearoom trade study (Humphreys, 1970) was met by strong reactions by both critics and supporters alike. The research was applauded by members of the gay community and some social scientists for shedding light on a little-known segment of our society, and for dispelling stereotypes and myths. Others, however, accused Humphreys of failing to protect his subjects' right to privacy, increasing their vulnerability to police detection, and deceiving his subjects about his true identity. Some faculty members at Washington University were so outraged by the research methods employed that they demanded (unsuccessfully) that Humphreys's doctoral degree be revoked.

A number of ethical questions were raised by the tearoom trade study, including whether a researcher is justified in acting contrary to the best interests of subjects in attempts to obtain valuable knowledge, to what extent deception is justified by the importance of an investigation, how one might go about studying illegal behavior in scientifically valid and ethically justifiable ways, and so on (see Sieber, 1982b). In this example, the conflict between the interests of scientists in obtaining knowledge and the interests of society in the protection of privacy and other rights is readily apparent.

## SUMMARY

The case studies described in this chapter reveal the complex nature of social science research. The ethical issues they raise often provide impediments to scientific progress oriented toward the betterment of the human social condition; they need not, however, result in exasperation among social researchers. Reviewing case studies of ethical dilemmas compels one to contemplate how such problems arise, and to consider potential solutions that do not seriously impair either the validity of an investigation or the respect for its participants (Sieber, 1982b).

Some of the major themes that will be considered in the following chapters also are revealed in the case studies, including the issues of deception and research participants' rights to privacy and informed consent (Chapter 4); special problems for the collection of longitudinal data (Chapter 5); potential harms of public disclosure of research findings (Chapter 5); and divergence of interests among researcher, subject, and institutions (Chapters 6 and 7). The challenge in the remainder of this book is to present and interpret the issues clearly enough so that their complexity becomes somewhat easier to unravel, and potential solutions to ethical dilemmas somewhat less impossible to envision.

## RECOMMENDED READINGS

Horowitz, I. L. (1967). *The rise and fall of Project Camelot*. Cambridge: MIT Press.
Humphreys, L. (1970). *Tearoom trade*. Chicago: Aldine.
McCord, J. (1978). A thirty-year follow-up of treatment effects. *American Psychologist, 33*, 284-289.
Rivlin, A. M., & Timpane, P. M. (Eds.). (1975). *Ethical and legal issues of social experimentation*. Washington, DC: Brookings Institution.
Sjoberg, G. (1967). Project Camelot: Selected reactions and personal reflections. In G. Sjoberg (Ed.), *Ethics, politics, and social research*. Cambridge, MA: Schenkman.
Vidich, A. J., & Bensman, J. (1958). *Small town in mass society: Class, power, and religion in a rural community*. Princeton, NJ: Princeton University Press.

## CHAPTER EXERCISES

*Discussion Questions.* Before proceeding on to Chapter 2, consider and respond to the following questions. Hold on to your answers, and refer back to them later as you complete the book. You may find your opinions changing as you are informed by subsequent chapters.

1. What should be the proper role of the applied social researcher? What types of research questions should be considered proper for directing the research efforts of applied social researchers?
2. What are the potential ethical conflicts that must be considered *before* an investigation is conducted?
3. What strategies can be employed to increase the researcher's autonomy from the administrative-control sector of large organizations?

4. Should Vidich and Bensman have gone ahead with the publication of their book about "Springdale" upon learning that some participants could be identified? What other courses of action could they have taken to protect the anonymity of the people in Springdale?

5. Should Laud Humphreys have been allowed to conduct his research on the "tearoom trade"? How might he have studied that segment of society without the use of deception?

# 2

# An Overview of Ethical
# Problems in Social Research

Although various attempts have been made to distinguish the characteristics of ethical problems in various types of applied research, such as
social experiments (Reynolds, 1979; Schelling, 1975), evaluation research
(Smith, 1985b), social intervention (Bermant, Kelman, & Warwick,
1978), and prevention research (Kimmel, 1985a), consensus appears to
be lacking among social researchers as to what actually constitutes an
ethical or moral issue in their investigations. A common confusion
apparently involves the distinction between "ethical" problems and
"moral" problems, and the point at which either constitutes a research
"dilemma." The sheer diversity of ethical problems that one might
encounter during the various stages of social research seems to have
precluded the emergence of a clear typology or set of classifying
characteristics by which to describe and contrast particular studies.

To the extent that clarity is lacking about the nature of the ethical
problems that typify applied studies and the terminology used in
describing them, it will be difficult for investigators to ensure that their
scientific endeavors are compatible with their values and goals. Thus
prior to a consideration of the existing ethical mechanisms for the
conduct of social research (Chapter 3) and an assessment of their impact
on research methodology (Chapter 4), the present chapter details how
one might identify an ethical problem, and describes the range of
problems that can arise. Initially, however, an attempt is made to clarify
the supposed distinction between the terms *ethical* and *moral*.

## ON BEING ETHICAL AND MORAL:
## IS THERE A DIFFERENCE?

"Ethics" and "morality" have similarly developed from terms that
pertain to customary or usual practice (Reese & Fremouw, 1984). The

word *ethics* is derived from the Greek *ethos*, meaning a person's character, nature, or disposition. It is defined in the *Oxford English Dictionary* (1933) as "relating to morals" (Vol. 3, p. 312) or, more specifically, "of or pertaining to the distinction between right and wrong or good and evil, in relation to actions, volitions, or character of responsible beings" (Vol. 6, p. 653). The synonym *morality* is derived from the Latin *moralis*, meaning custom, manners, or character. In essence, both ethics and morality refer to usual or normal behavior.

Consistent with these derivations, philosopher William Frankena (1973) defined *ethics* as a branch of philosophy that deals with thinking about morality, moral problems, and judgments of proper conduct. Frankena emphasized that while the terms ethical and moral both pertain to morality, they are not to be confused with morally right or morally good. A moral judgment thus is one that involves a matter of right or wrong, ought or ought not, a good action or a bad one. Whenever the question "Should I conduct this study?" is raised in social research, a moral issue is at stake.

Ethical problems are in fact moral problems, even though some people choose to use these terms as if a difference existed. In contrast to moral concerns, which question whether specific acts are consistent with accepted notions of right or wrong, the term *ethical* is used to connote rules of behavior or conformity to a code or set of principles (Frankena, 1973; Reynolds, 1979). To illustrate, one might maintain that a psychologist acted ethically in the sense of not having violated the profession's codified rules of proper behavior, but still feel that the behavior was immoral (Smith, 1985a). This assessment would not necessarily imply a distinction between the terms, but rather a difference in the principles used to judge the psychologist's behavior. The psychologist's behavior was viewed as being proper according to one set of principles (those by which professional psychologists are guided), but not according to another (a broader and more general set of moral principles). Thus the terms *ethical* and *moral* may be used interchangeably to refer to rules of proper conduct, although one may prefer to distinguish between them in a context where codified principles are relevant.

Because the terms *ethical* and *moral* are inevitably linked with values, they might more accurately be described as referring to behaviors about which society holds certain values (Reese & Fremouw, 1984). Generally speaking, a *value* is an expression of that which is valued or held important (Steininger et al., 1984). When moral problems reflect uncertainty about how to balance competing values it is proper to speak of the situation as an ethical or moral *dilemma* (Smith, 1985b). A dilemma is apparent in research situations in which two or more desirable values present themselves in a seemingly mutually exclusive way, with each value suggesting a different course of action that cannot be maximized simultaneously.

Most of the ethical issues discussed in this book are ones resulting from conflicting sets of values concerning the goals, processes, or outcomes of an investigation. For example, one very common dilemma in psychological research involving human participants arises from the fact that strict adherence to the ethical standards that currently face psychologists requires that they first obtain informed voluntary consent from their research participants. *Informed consent* is the procedure by which individuals choose whether or not to participate in an experiment after being presented with information that likely would affect their decision (American Psychological Association, 1982). The information presented typically includes an explanation of the nature of the experimental procedure and a specific elaboration of possible adverse reactions (Loftus & Fries, 1979). The moral justification for informed consent is that the individual who is to submit to research should be given full opportunity to exercise judgment in order to determine what will be done to his or her mind and body.

In many cases, informed consent is impractical, as in field studies of crowd behavior, helping behavior, littering patterns, and the like (Reese & Fremouw, 1984). In addition, for some time now, psychologists have known that their "test tubes" are dirty, in the sense that subjects come to experiments and try to figure out the investigator's hypotheses, thus increasing the probability of the investigator's predictions (Rosenthal & Rosnow, 1969). Thus if researchers had to provide subjects with full information about their experimental plans, procedures, and hypotheses, the resulting psychology of human behavior might very well be based on the kinds of behavior subjects think experimenters are looking for.

Confronted by the problems inherent in the measurement process, whereby the act of observing individuals alters the responses being measured (technically known as "observational reactivity"), it is easy to understand why a psychologist may feel tempted to mislead subjects about the true nature of the experiment. In revealing the exact substance of the research, the psychologist runs the risk of distorting subjects' reactions and ultimately limiting the applicability of the findings. Thus behavioral scientists who wish to be open and straightforward with their subjects, but realize that to do so might jeopardize the validity of their research findings, are faced with an ethical dilemma. They are forced to weigh the ethical importance of informed consent against the scientific requirements of validity and to decide which violation constitutes the lesser evil (Rosenthal & Rosnow, 1975). (See Chapter 4 for further consideration of the informed consent dilemma.)

Another illustration of an ethical dilemma in social research involves the *labeling effect*, which poses a particularly serious impasse for prevention researchers (Kimmel, 1985a). It is a very common strategy in the preventive intervention movement to achieve early identification of persons at risk, and to modify their environments so as to reduce that risk. This necessitates alerting significant persons in the environment of their *at-risk* status, persons who are also in other ways important reinforcers and gatekeepers in their lives, such as teachers, parents, employers, and perhaps peers. With the label *at risk* so widely distributed, or signified by attendance at special classes or treatment sessions, their preneurotic or prepsychotic status becomes public knowledge. Further complicating this situation is the potential conflict a researcher might face when labeling an individual enables that person to get special services. Certain agencies and institutions require labeling (according to the *Diagnostic and Statistics Manual of the American Psychiatric Association III*) before services will be given. The ethical dilemma that emerges is the conflict between helping the at-risk individual by assigning a negative label and not qualifying that person for help by not assigning a label (Carroll, Schneider, & Wesley, 1985). While the researcher typically is not the labeler, or the person doing the alerting, it can be argued that it is his or her moral responsibility to protect research participants from labeling effects.

It is easy to anticipate that the cumulative mental health damage from the labeling effect would often far outweigh the special preventive interventions received. Children in classrooms who are labeled as high-risk delinquents or drug abusers, may become victims of self-fulfilling prophesies in rating and grading, stereotyping, scapegoating, destructive teasing, name calling, and so on. Designing intervention studies that minimize or avoid the labeling and stigmatizing process represents a way that these potentially negative unintended effects of prevention research might be counteracted. (Research designs for reducing the likelihood of labeling effects are described in Chapter 4.)

## CHARACTERISTICS OF ETHICAL
## PROBLEMS IN SOCIAL RESEARCH

Any attempt to clarify the nature of ethical problems in social research requires that their characteristics first be identified. An initial such attempt was made by Smith (1985b) who, in his analysis of an actual incident in evaluation research, identified several characteristics of moral problems in applied science. Social research evaluators are often confronted with ethical problems because they assume responsibility for determining what is beneficial in social programs and policies. In addition, their work can be influential in terms of who receives the benefits and pays the costs of the social programs, and such suggestions for the redistribution of funds invariably raise ethical questions pertaining to proper conduct. Smith's illustrative case study provides a useful starting point for obtaining a deeper and more general understanding of the nature of ethical problems in social research.

The incident analyzed by Smith involved a private research and development firm's evaluation of a federally funded project intended to increase reading and mathematics skills in a high-crime, poor, inner-city school district. Following a thorough study of the curriculum materials and a considerable amount of time spent on the site, the firm's evaluation unit sent a final report directly to the federal agency and the school district without administrative review, as the firm had no formal review procedure. The school district officials and local residents were strongly critical of the report because it contained a lengthy description of the context of the study that, they argued, threatened to destroy their district's image. When these protests eventually reached the director of the research and development firm, the evaluation study's finding were covered up, the evaluation unit manager was fired, and members of the evaluation staff were transferred within the firm or else resigned. The director then hired a senior external evaluation consultant to review the entire incident.

The external consultant determined that the data presented in the report, although accurate, were overly detailed and that the report seemed to lack balance. In the consultant's view, readily available information on the positive aspects of the school district should have been included along with the extensive negative information, and the contextual description of the school district should have been related to the process or outcomes of the program. Some time later, the central evaluation unit was disbanded by the firm's director and replaced with evaluators who worked on separate projects. Although this dismantling had been already in progress, the consultant felt that his review of the report probably gave the director further impetus for that action, and perhaps contributed to the burying of important information that could have improved the district's educational program.

In analyzing this case in order to identify its moral characteristics, perhaps the first aspect that becomes apparent is the overall complexity of the incident. Indeed, *multiple ethical issues can be represented in a single social research situation.* Several ethical questions can be asked about this single evaluation incident, including whether it was proper for (1) the evaluation unit to produce an unbalanced report; (2) the evaluation unit manager to release the report without preliminary feedback from the evaluated school officials; (3) evaluation reports to be disseminated by the firm without a formal review procedure; and (4) the firm's director to fire the evaluation manager, disband the centralized evaluation unit, and hire an outside consultant to review the report and subsequent actions taken.

The likelihood that multiple ethical questions will emerge within a given situation demonstrates how important it is for an investigator to maintain caution in attempting to isolate *the* ethical question within a single research problem. One also must be sensitive to the possible consequences of any action taken, since a response to one aspect of an ethical dilemma may, at the same time, exacerbate or give rise to other unanticipated, troublesome issues.

In addition to the complexity of ethical issues, Smith identified several other ethical characteristics illustrated by the evaluation incident, and, like the first, these characteristics appear to generalize to a wide variety of social research investigations. For example, it is apparent in the evaluation case that *ethical sensitivity does not, in and of itself, guarantee that an ethical problem will be sufficiently resolved.* Although one might question whether the evaluation unit manager was too inexperienced to foresee the potential consequences of the evaluation report, or else insensitive to the feelings of the district's residents, it is clear that the firm's director and the external consultant were concerned about the extent to which their behaviors were proper. Ethical sensitivity was necessary for the director and the consultant to raise important questions, but not sufficient for them to choose the most satisfactory course of action.

The incident also illustrates a point made earlier, that *conflicting values tend to give rise to ethical problems.* In this situation, the unit manager perhaps felt that the value of fully disclosing the contextual information outweighed the value of protecting the district from potential risks. The research and development firm's director had to weigh the competing values of protecting the firm's reputation versus supporting the firm's employees, and learning the "truth" about the quality of the evaluation report versus protecting the firm from further criticism. The consultant was faced with the competing values of making an objective assessment of the evaluation report versus supporting the firm's evaluation process. For each dilemma, a compromise perhaps could have been reached in such a way as to satisfy the competing values (e.g., the director might have found a way to protect the firm's reputation without firing the unit manager). However, each set of conflicting values in part represented the source of disagreement about proper ethical conduct.

Another characteristic of an ethical problem identified by Smith is that *ethical questions can relate both to the conduct of the research and the subject matter of the research*. Whereas much attention has been focused on the appropriateness of actions taken by social researchers, such as the protection of participants' anonymity and confidentiality of data, less emphasis has been placed on the actual nature of the programs researched. One can question the ethical acceptability of the focus of the research (e.g., a program that is evaluated) as well as the ethical acceptability of the conduct of the research (e.g., the evaluation process itself). In the evaluation incident, ethical issues pertaining to the educational program studied are as pertinent as the ethical issues pertaining to the conduct and consequences of the evaluation. An educational program that succeeds in enhancing students' cognitive skills can, at the same time, reinforce their dependency on special recognition and privileges. (Recall that this latter point was offered as a possible explanation for the unanticipated consequences of the Cambridge-Somerville Study.) The nature of some investigations in prevention can give rise to similar ethical questions, as when a prevention study is implemented contrary to the desires or concerns of the targeted recipients of the intervention. Certain mental health programs, as well, have been questioned in terms of the various political implications inherent in helping people adjust to unjust conditions and emphasizing what individuals can do for themselves (Muñoz, 1983).

An ethical problem also can be described by the fact that *determinations about proper conduct often require a broad perspective*. An adequate judgment of the appropriateness of an action sometimes can be more easily reached if information about its consequences is available. At times, a more complete understanding of an ethical problem can only come about when actions are considered in retrospect, and from a broader perspective than available during the conduct of an investigation. An assessment about whether the evaluation director behaved properly by disbanding the evaluation unit perhaps would be affected by an awareness that the evaluators who stayed on were sensitized to the importance of protecting the rights of their participants, thereby improving the quality (and ethical acceptability) of their work. While such retrospective assessments hardly are useful to a social scientist in the initial decision-making situation, they can improve the quality of subsequent decisions (Smith, 1985b). However, to say that the understanding of an ethical problem requires a historical perspective and the accumulation of practical experience is not meant to imply that moral judgments can be ascertained *only* through a reliance on the consequences of an action. The latter reflects an ethical position known as *utilitarianism*, which is described in the next chapter.

Another identifying characteristic noted by Smith is that *an ethical problem involves both personal and professional elements.* When scientists disagree over questions concerning the potential hazards of a particular procedure, effects of deception on subjects' suspiciousness, the effects of confidentiality procedures on survey return rates and subject participation, and so on, the disagreements are not of conflicting personal concerns but of scientific opinion, which changes as knowledge is gained. Professional values are largely guided and maintained by the established ethical principles and procedures of a profession. In addition to this professional aspect of ethical problems is a personal aspect, which motivates decision making based on one's own conscience. In the evaluation incident, the director's decision to fire the evaluation manager, and the consultant's decision about his proper role, were no doubt highly personal ones. Clearly, ethical decision making involves elements that are both subjective and objective in nature, consisting of "a mixture of knowledge and opinion, science and moral preferences" (Confrey, 1970, p. 530). Ethical judgments might be based on a motivating factor, such as the pride a scientist derives from a major accomplishment, or a factor reflecting level of sophistication in terms of an awareness of the ethical issues and professional standards of proper conduct (see Chapter 7).

Other distinguishing characteristics of ethical problems in social research can be added to those suggested by Smith. For example, because personal values may play a significant role in scientific investigations, researchers must be careful to protect the integrity of their inquiries through careful data collection and analysis, and accurate and objective reporting of their research findings. Reese and Fremouw (1984) have argued that *ethical problems can pertain to the "ethics of science" (i.e., the protection of the integrity of data) or the "ethics of research" (i.e., the protection of human rights).* The ethics of research is related to the means and social consequences of the discovery of scientific truths; an unethical judgment can thereby undermine the rights of research participants through the methods used, or society at large through the implications of the research findings. On the other hand, the ethics of science deals with normative rules that protect the integrity of data ("integrity" in the sense of intellectual, rather than moral, soundness). In that the ethics of science is related to scientific truth per se, an unethical judgment can potentially undermine science as a body of knowledge. This distinction is an important one for identifying an ethical problem in research in which the risks are not necessarily to society, but that instead pose threats to the scientific community, as is the case when personal and subjective biases directly or indirectly distort the accuracy of a research report.

When attempting to describe ethical problems, it is important to recognize that *the distinction between ethical and unethical behavior is not dichotomous,* even though the normative code of prescribed ("ought") and proscribed ("ought not") behaviors, as represented by the ethical standards of a profession, seem to imply that it is. According to Reese and Fremouw (1984), judgments about whether a behavior violates professional values lie on a continuum that ranges from the clearly unethical to the clearly ethical. When an ethical problem arises, it is not uncommon to find a divergence between the expressed (normative) ethical standards and actual behavioral practices (see Childress, 1975).

In essence, ethical principles usually are not absolute, but must be interpreted in light of the research context, and of other values at stake. For example, although psychology's ethical standards (American Psychological Association, 1981a, 1982) dictate that informed consent be obtained whenever possible, the realities of the research situation may render this normative requirement as a mere guideline from which some degree of deviation is necessary. The use of *deception*—the deliberate withholding of, or misinforming about, important information—usually is seen as permissible as long as certain conditions are met (such as when no alternative means of investigation are available, risks are minimal, and adequate debriefing is provided). As described earlier, the nature of certain scientific questions of interest to researchers might require the use of deception in order to protect the validity of participants' responses. Deception represents a potential violation of participants' rights, but without its use certain questions could not be investigated through valid research. However, the mere fact that a practice flourishes should not be taken as evidence that it is morally acceptable. That people lie, cheat, and steal are not moral defenses for those practices. That social researchers often deceive their subjects is not a defense of that practice.

A final point, and one that is often overlooked in contrasting or identifying ethical issues, is that *ethical problems can arise from the decision to conduct research and the decision not to conduct the research.* Ethical assessments of social research traditionally have considered the costs and utilities of conducting a particular study, but often have failed to address the costs (and utilities) of *not* conducting the study (Rosenthal & Rosnow, 1984). A researcher might be reluctant to conduct a particular investigation, or perhaps is critical of someone else's research, because the procedure is contrary to the established standards of good scientific practice. At the same time, the decision *not* to conduct the research can run contrary to the best interests of research participants or other members of society. Thus a psychologist who refuses to do a study because it involves an invasion of subjects' privacy, but that, if conducted, might reduce violence or prejudice, has not solved an ethical problem, but has merely traded one problem for another (Rosenthal & Rosnow, 1984).

The decision not to investigate a scientific problem because it carries a certain cost is to be evaluated on ethical grounds as surely as the decision to conduct the study. However, this evaluation is complicated by the fact that research questions typically can be pursued in more than one manner. In addition, most moral philosophers would agree that avoiding harms that are immediate and certain may be more important than conferring benefits that are uncertain and distant in time (see Levine, 1975b; Natanson, 1975). Thus the decision to do or not to do a study is a complex one, and poses a challenge for the researcher to select methods that preserve both scientific validity and morality. (See Chapter 8 for a fuller consideration of this issue.)

The nature of ethical problems in social research no doubt could be described by a far more extensive list of characteristics than that presented here. The nine characteristics identified here are intended to focus attention on some of the more important aspects of ethical difficulties worthy of consideration and study, and may be apparent at all levels of research activity. To summarize, ethical problems in social research will have some of the following characteristics:

(1) The complexity of a single research problem can give rise to multiple questions of proper behavior.
(2) Sensitivity to ethical issues is necessary but not sufficient for solving them.
(3) Ethical problems are the results of conflicting values.
(4) Ethical problems can relate to both the subject matter of the research and the conduct of the research.
(5) An adequate understanding of an ethical problem sometimes requires a broad perspective based on the consequences of research.
(6) Ethical problems involve both personal and professional elements.
(7) Ethical problems can pertain to science (as a body of knowledge) and to research (conducted in such a way as to protect the rights of society and research participants).
(8) Judgments about proper conduct lie on a continuum ranging from the clearly unethical to the clearly ethical.
(9) An ethical problem can be encountered as a result of a decision to conduct a particular study or a decision not to conduct the study.

## TYPOLOGY OF ETHICAL PROBLEMS
## IN APPLIED SOCIAL RESEARCH

Ethical problems can be categorized and contrasted according to the level of the research process that they most directly affect. It is suggested that the following three levels also represent a typology of ethical problems in applied social research: (1) the individual research participants who are actively involved in the research, (2) the society in and/or for which the research is conducted, and (3) the body of scientific knowledge to which the results and conclusions are incorporated.

*Social research and the individual research participants.* When ethical problems are viewed at the level of the individual participants of research, special attention should be paid to the nature of the relationship between the investigator and the individuals who provide the research data. As Kelman (1972) has argued, there is an inevitable power discrepancy inherent in the social role of the researcher due, in large part, to his or her specialized knowledge and responsibility in defining the conditions of the research. Subjects for social research tend to be drawn from the relatively powerless segments of society, such as from lower-status positions in organizations where research is conducted, and from less affluent communities. Their disadvantage is exacerbated within the structure of the research situation itself. This power differential, according to Kelman, leaves subjects with less freedom to refuse research participation, and less leverage to protect themselves against procedures they find objectionable and that may be contrary to their own interests.

It is not surprising that the term *subject* has taken on a pejorative meaning. Throughout early history, subjects were subservient to the divine rights of kings. In medical usage, the term represents a cadaver that is dissected for anatomical study or exhibition. The current trend to supersede "subject" with "participant" to characterize an individual who participates in research seems to suggest more of an equality of the role relationships in research, and perhaps implies a readiness by researchers to do without a certain degree of status (Schuler, 1982). Nevertheless, individuals who enter into a research situation become involved in a relationship structured unlike usual interactions, and risk placing their fate in the hands of a researcher whom they are confident will respect their welfare (Orne, 1962). This situation is particularly acute for individuals who are dependent and powerless by virtue of their age, physical and mental condition, or social deviance—such as children and the elderly, mental patients, and criminals.

In terms of its undesirable effects on participants, social research, at least in the past, has been relatively innocuous, especially when compared to alleged medical abuses in some situations (see, for example, Beecher, 1966). However, subjects for social research risk the following sorts of undesirable effects or "damages": (1) actual changes in their characteristics, such as physical health, attitudes, personality, and self-concept; (2) an experience that creates tension or anxiety; (3) collection of "private" information that might embarrass them or make them liable to legal action if made public; (4) receiving unpleasant information about themselves that they might not otherwise have to confront; and (5) invasion of privacy through the collection of certain types of damaging information (Levine, 1975b; Reynolds, 1972). Such damages are moderated by the degree of identification of the subjects (to the investigators, to themselves individually, and to each other as a group), by the way in which they will be reported on in the study, and by the consequences of identification (Schelling, 1975).

Ethical problems at the participant level become particularly acute as the role relationship between subject and investigator loses a semblance of equality and, concurrently, as the legitimacy in the use of power is lost by the investigator. According to Kelman (1972), the legitimate use of power in a research setting can occur when researchers maintain more of a partnership with their research participants, sharing common norms and values with them that define the limits and conditions of the usage of power. In addition, those individuals over whom power is exercised in research should have recourse to certain mechanisms—such as courts and ethics committees—through which they can question or complain about the way in which the power is used.

*Social research and society.* Special care must be taken to protect the rights of the public at large so that they are not jeopardized by the social consequences of research discoveries or by the publication of research results. There are a number of desirable, albeit general, outcomes potentially resulting from social research for collectivities of individuals (such as improvements in social position, health, education, and working conditions), and for society as a whole (such as an increase in knowledge and an ability to control biomedical, psychological, and social phenomena). Certain studies, however, are designed to gather information that, at least in the short term, may be viewed by members of the subject population as being against their best interests. For example, there may be a strong group interest in denying information that is sought in research designed to control public smoking, pilferage in work settings, breaking speed laws, littering, access to pornography, and the like (Schelling, 1975).

Ethical problems at the societal level can involve more subtle effects (Reynolds, 1979). Members of a society might experience a reduced sense of personal autonomy as knowledge of phenomena increases, and questions about the trustworthiness of those responsible for applying new knowledge might emerge. Other subtle negative consequences can be identified when the focus of research involves social systems, as is often the case in such disciplines as anthropology, political science, sociology, and economics. An investigation that successfully enhances the task effectiveness of a social system can do so at the expense of individual rights, and might have unforeseen consequences, such as the promotion of organized crime. Levin (1981) has contrasted the ethical issues involved in much sociological research, where patterns of behavior that characterize social structure are studied, with psychological research concerned with individual differences or situational determinants of behavior. Sociological research, unlike its psychological counterpart, can be characterized by its attempt to explain phenomena of the social structure that influence large numbers of individuals. According to Levin, research into the social order of a community, organization, or entire society frequently uncovers evidence of publicly unacknowledged forms of activity, such as white-collar crime, shady business practices, political corruption, and organizational ineptitude. As such, what may be viewed as an invasion of privacy in a psychological study "can be regarded in sociological research as no less than subversive activity that undermines social institutions by exposing their frailties" (Levin, 1981, p. 52). Thus in order for research on social structure and change to make an important scientific contribution, it may be necessary to exceed certain standards and risk, raising thorny ethical issues.

*Social research and scientific knowledge.* A wide range of ethical problems are inherent in the collection, analysis, and reporting of social research data. Although it is assumed that the data collected by social researchers will have intellectual integrity or trustworthiness, data can be manipulated in various ways to undermine the accumulation of knowledge in a scientific discipline. As first suggested by Babbage (1969), violations can include "cooking" (the selection of only those data that fit the research hypothesis), "trimming" (the manipulation of data to make them look better), or "forging" (the complete fabrication of data). Attempts at replication can serve to correct the harm to science caused by such violations, but such attempts may be especially rare for large-scale social research investigations that are prohibitively expensive (Fisher, 1982).

When scientists enter applied areas, they must almost always change their frame of reference. The ethics of scientific investigations are, in part, to observe and report all data accurately and completely, even if one of the scientist's treasured theories is threatened by such reporting. The social researcher who enters into an adversary situation (including research positions for private businesses, governmental agencies, and so forth) confronts a different ethical situation than the scientist who conducts research in the "ivory tower."

In the former case, data that are gathered may not be made public in a purely or fully objective way. For example, a researcher hired and paid by an organization is expected by that organization to work in its best interest. As such, the researcher faces certain inevitable constraints and is placed in a position of vulnerability in having to balance organizational loyalty and professional objectivity (Adams, 1985). There may be pressure to downplay negative (and emphasize positive) findings as they reflect on the organization's programs and operations. There might also be reinforcement for engaging in nonthreatening research activities, and a reduced access to confidential and sensitive information that could severely impede the research process.

Ethical problems can emerge at some point beyond the actual data-collection stage of the research process. Perhaps the most troubling effects of scientific data arise when new knowledge is misused or when widely accepted procedures and principles with proven utility are improperly implemented. The inappropriate utilization of research findings outside clearly stated boundary conditions can have serious and far-reaching methodological and ethical consequences. This, in turn, raises some important questions about the ethics of generalizability and applied, cross-disciplinary research (that is, research situations in which scientists consult with and report their data to private businesses, governmental departments, commercial agencies, etc.).

Another ethical problem pertinent to scientific knowledge concerns whether or not the public is better served by withholding research results until they are released in a peer-reviewed journal, or by reporting them in detail as early as possible (Bermel, 1985). Both approaches have potential drawbacks: The early reporting of research findings can hinder public understanding if the report lacks critical information and can be misinterpreted, while long delays in peer-reviewed publication can result in the withholding of information for those who deserve to hear of the results as quickly as possible. Sommer and Sommer (1983) have expressed their concern regarding the ease with which tentative information becomes widespread in textbooks and the technical literature, since summary reports often permit the misinterpretation of actual research findings. These and related issues, which concern a researcher's responsibility for making clear the limitations of the evidence he or she presents, are considered in detail in Chapter 6.


## SUMMARY


Ethical problems in social research reflect concerns about proper conduct related to the processes and consequences of research and procedure. These ethical problems can be identified by a number of characteristics, and classified into a typology according to the level of the research process at which they have their clearest implications, including the treatment of research participants, responsibility to society, and integrity in the collection, analysis, and reporting of data.

## RECOMMENDED READINGS

Bermant, G., Kelman, H. C., & Warwick, D. P. (1978). *The ethics of social intervention.* Washington, DC: Hemisphere.

Katz, J. (1972). *Experimentation with human beings.* New York: Russell Sage.

National Commission for the Protection of Human Subjects of Biomedical and Behavioral Research (1975). *Appendix, Vols. I and II: The Belmont Report.* Bethesda, MD: Department of Health, Education and Welfare.

Sigma Xi, The Scientific Research Society. (1984). *Honor in science.* New Haven, CT: Author.

Smith, N. L. (Ed.). (1985). Special issue: Moral and ethical problems in evaluation. In *Evaluation and Program Planning, 8.* New York: Pergamon.

## CHAPTER EXERCISES

1. Consider the evaluation research incident described in the chapter. What potential ethical problems can you identify at the (a) participant, (b) societal, and (c) scientific knowledge levels?

2. *Case Study*: Describe the ethical problems posed by the following example of applied social research:

> A research program has been planned to determine means for reducing, and ultimately preventing, the negative consequences of divorce (such as a reduced ability to function, self-condemnation, and traumatic effects on children). The research will involve extensive psychological testing and in-depth interviews with recently divorced individuals, including those who have suffered adverse effects and those who have successfully avoided, or else successfully coped with, undesirable effects. The researchers intend to report their study in a scientific journal, and hope that implications drawn from their findings will be applied in a variety of counseling and training contexts.

# 3

# Ethical Standards and
# Guidelines for Social Research

As an expression of our values and a guide to achieving them, research ethics help to ensure that our scientific endeavors are compatible with our values and goals, through shared guidelines, principles, and written and unwritten laws. In this chapter, a representative sample of ethical theories upon which individual moral reasoning and professional codes of ethics are based is described. The chapter then compares and contrasts professional ethical codes with governmental regulation of research with human participants, and examines the impact that professional ethical codes and governmental regulations have had on each other during the last several years.

## ETHICAL THEORIES
## AND MORAL REASONING

Because people differ in terms of their general approaches to ethical decision making, it is important in science for researchers to be aware of which theory they endorse and which takes precedence when there is a moral dilemma. The essential differences between ethical positions are found in the extent to which the determination of the goodness of an action depends upon that action's consequences, and in the rules used for handling competing principles in a situation (Bunda, 1985).

Prior to a consideration of the different approaches to ethical decision making, a distinction between *normative ethics* and *metaethics* needs to be clarified. This distinction underlies much of the disagreement among philosophers as to the precise scope of ethics (Sahakian, 1974). Some philosophers believe that ethics should provide a set of principles to guide human behavior, whereas others argue instead that ethics should present an analysis of the statements made by people when they express moral beliefs. The former describes the approach taken by some adherents of normative ethics, which set forth standards by which people may judge the morality of actions; the latter represents the approach taken by metaethical philosophers who study the logic, semantics, and epistemology of ethical theories, apart from the study of ethical and moral conduct (Titus & Keeton, 1973).

The primary concern of normative ethics is to guide individuals in their attempts to make decisions and judgments about proper actions in particular situations (Frankena, 1973). According to this view, moral principles can be established on a rationally justifiable basis through the investigation of moral theories. As such, normative ethics set forth moral norms that indicate what one should do or refrain from doing in various circumstances. Some ethicists assert that these norms reflect objective moral truths that reveal one's obligations, responsibilities, and correct moral conduct. According to Frankena (1973, p. 12), the primary question in the area of normative ethics is "how may or should we decide or determine what is morally right for a certain agent . . . to do, or what he morally ought to do, in a certain situation?"

In opposition to normative views, metaethical philosophers argue that attempts to reveal moral truths and establish principles of correct moral conduct interfere with a person's freedom to make his or her own moral choices. Rather than attempting to construct a systematic theory of ethics for daily living, such philosophers are concerned instead with the analysis or logic of moral concepts. Metaethics focuses on the question of how (if at all) ethical and value judgments can be established or justified, the nature of morality, the meaning of expressions such as "morally right" or "good," and other similar concerns (Frankena, 1973). Because metaethics considers what "good" or "right" means rather than what is good or bad, right or wrong, it poses questions *about* the normative judgments that are made (Garner & Rosen, 1967). For metaethical philosophers, an ethical theory is not to be viewed as a set of suggestions that guide our moral judgments, but rather as "an attempt to show what people are doing when they make moral judgments" (Ayer, 1963, p. 246).

As described by Frankena (1973, p. 12), normative theories of moral conduct "guide us in our capacity as agents trying to decide what we should do in this case and in that" and also assist us in advising, instructing, and judging the actions of others. As such, a consideration of normative theories of ethics can be helpful in evaluating problems about what is right or ought to be done relevant to the actions or goals of social research. Although metaethical questions pertaining to the meaning and justification of one's ethical judgments are not the concern of this book, it should be kept in mind that such questions need to be considered before one can be entirely satisfied with the normative theory that he or she uses as the basis for research decisions (Frankena, 1973).

In general, research choices are based on two sorts of ethical theories that commonly enter into discussions of moral problems—*teleological* and *deontological* theories (Frankena, 1973). A teleological theory of ethics holds an action as morally right or obligatory if it or the rule under which it falls will produce the greatest possible balance of good over evil. For teleologists, the consequences of an act determine its value—an act is considered morally right if it leads to better consequences (i.e., a greater balance of good over evil) than any alternative act. In contrast, deontological theorists contend that considerations other than consequences must be taken into account in moral judgments. A deontological theory of ethics holds that what makes an action or adoption of a rule right depends on more than simply the balance of good over evil produced. The term *deontology* has evolved from the Greek *deon* (duty) and *logos* (science and reason), suggesting that certain acts are to be viewed as morally right or obligatory not because of their effects on human welfare, but rather because they keep a promise, show gratitude, demonstrate loyalty to an unconditional command, and the like.

A variety of ethical positions have emerged within the teleological and deontological orientations, and the lines of distinction between these positions sometimes tend to blur. For the sake of simplicity, the descriptions that follow are brief and do not consider the various theories in their total complexity, nor is there an attempt to summarize fully the objections commonly raised against them.

## Teleological Theories

While teleologists agree that the ethicality of an act should be judged by its consequences, there are differing opinions about the decisive features of consequences. One way that teleologists differ can be found in their views about what consequences ought to be regarded as good or evil. Some teleologists are hedonists who emphasize the pleasure or happiness that can be derived from an action; others instead look to the survival value of behaviors, while others stress the realization of individual potentialities as the basis for judging the goodness of consequences (Titus & Keeton, 1973). In short, teleologists hold some view about what it is that is conducive to the greatest good, whether it be pleasure, power, knowledge, or perfection, and so on.

Teleologists also differ in terms of whose welfare ought to be promoted by the balance of good over evil. For example, the focus of teleological considerations might be one's own good, the good of one's family, nation, class, or the good of the world as a whole. *Ethical egoism* is a teleological theory that considers the greatest well-being of "the agent alone" (i.e., the best interests of the individual who is making the moral judgment), and not all persons affected. The philosophies of Nietzsche, Hobbes, and Epicurus are representative examples of this view. Ethical egoists maintain that a person's conduct or rule of action "is right if and only if it promotes at least as great a balance of good over evil for him in the long run as any alternative would, and wrong if it does not" (Frankena, 1973, p. 15).

The teleological position known as *utilitarianism* (or *ethical universalism*) asserts that an activity or rule of conduct is right if, and only if, it produces the greatest well-being of *everyone* affected by it. The clearest statement of utilitarianism is presented in John Stuart Mill's (1957) *principle of utility*, the ethical principle that an individual ought to do that act that promotes the greatest good, happiness, or satisfaction for the most people. Utilitarians maintain that an individual considering alternative moral choices must consider the full, net consequences of each of the available alternative actions. In utilitarian considerations, no one person's happiness, such as that of the individual decision maker, is to be held as more important than another's. Each person in the aggregate counts as one, and no more than one, in the determination of an act's consequences.

By taking the potential welfare of all individuals into account when deciding on the proper course of action, utilitarians would argue that social science research should be directed toward the elimination of such social ills as racism, rape, child abuse, and so on, and that the use of human subjects to attain this goal is justified on utilitarian grounds (Atwell, 1981). (Of course, utilitarians might urge instead that money be redirected away from research and used to improve the human condition in a more direct and immediate way, namely, by feeding the hungry, providing shelter for the homeless, and the like.)

A major criticism of the utilitarian approach in research contexts is that by basing ethical judgments on a utilitarian cost-benefit analysis, a researcher might be easily convinced that the long-range benefits to society of deceptive, manipulative research outweigh the short-range costs to participants who are deceived (Baumrind, 1985). Such objections typically are based on the deontological belief that the ethics of human research should be governed by the proposition that individuals are ends in and of themselves and must not figure as means to an end beyond their own interest (see below). In this view, research participants are believed to have certain inalienable rights that cannot be violated for pragmatic reasons, such as for the accumulation of scientifically derived knowledge. Utilitarians, by contrast, would argue that scientific ends sometimes justify the use of means that would necessarily sacrifice individual subjects' welfare, particularly when the research promises the "greatest good for the greatest number." Such an approach is a modern variant of the moral suggestion that the end (e.g., the advancement of knowledge) sometimes justifies the means (e.g., deceit or risk of harm). Despite objections to the utilitarian approach for resolving ethical dilemmas, it appears that most people, when faced with moral issues, do tend to consider the consequences their actions might have on others (Steininger et al., 1984).

Falling somewhere between ethical egoism and utilitarianism are other teleological theories that judge the rightness or wrongness of acts according to what promotes the greatest good for a certain group, such as one's family, class, nation, or race. This third kind of view and ethical egoism have been labeled "restricted" teleological theories by Broad (1930) to distinguish them from utilitarianism, which encompasses *all* persons and not any individual, political, or institutional boundary.

**Deontological Theories**

In contrast to the teleological focus on consequences in considerations of an action's rightness or wrongness, a deontological theory of ethics holds that at least some basic actions are good in and of themselves without regard to whether they maximize some consequences. Deontologists do not contend that consequences should not matter at all, but rather that certain conduct is right-making or wrong-making irrespective of the consequences. That is, a deontologist might view an action or rule as right even though it does not maximize the greatest balance of good over evil for certain individuals. Deontologists, like teleologists, often differ in their views about what is good or right; however, they either do not hold the balance of consequences as a moral criterion or else minimize its importance in ethical judgments.

For the most part, deontological theories can be distinguished by the role they assign to general rules (Frankena, 1973). *Rule-deontological theories* represent the view that particular judgments or decisions about what is right or wrong can be derived from general principles or rules.

For rule-deontologists, general principles or rules are basic in morality, or at least more binding than the rules of thumb or general maxims that are derived from past experience (Frankena & Granrose, 1974). This position suggests that a general rule, such as "One should always tell the truth" would always hold, whereas a rule of thumb may not always be appropriate in particular situations. For example, a sociologist might decide on the basis of past experience conducting research to deceive research participants about the true purpose of a study, with the hope that a subsequent debriefing session will alleviate any harms the procedure may cause (such as loss of self-esteem in the subject who has been fooled by the deception, increased suspiciousness among participants about social research, and so on). By relying on the rule of thumb that deception may be necessary in certain studies to obtain accurate data from research participants, the sociologist has made an exception to the general standard of informed consent. From a rule-deontological perspective, a more appropriate course of action would be to obtain subjects' informed consent in such instances, even though it would be more convenient to do without it, and even though the research goal is a worthy one.

The sociologist in the above example may well be characterized as an *act-deontologist*. In the most extreme version of act-deontologism, it is held that moral judgments must be made separately in each particular situation, without an appeal to general rules and without a concern about what actions will maximize good over evil consequences. Ethical conduct for act-deontologists is derived from particular judgments, such as "In this situation, such and such should be done" (Frankena, 1973). A less extreme form of act-deontologism contends that general rules may evolve from particular cases and be useful for guiding subsequent decisions; however, this position holds that general rules should never supersede a particular judgment in guiding behavior. Both forms of act-deontologism described here are often referred to as *situation ethics*.

Some examples of deontological theories of ethics are represented in the positions of philosophers Immanuel Kant, W. D. Ross, and John Rawls. The moral views of Kant (1965) are closely associated with rule-deontologism. Kant emphasized the importance of moral laws as *categorical imperatives*—principles of behavior that define appropriate action in all situations and to which adherence is expected as a matter of duty. In Kant's view, categorical imperatives are universally applicable in relevantly similar cases. An act is held as morally justifiable if, and only if, one is willing to have anyone else behave in a like manner in similar circumstances. In addition, right carries with it a sense of duty, and this alone justifies behaving independently of an action's consequences. The principle of justice or truth, for example, stands by itself as a rule of behavior that is right, without recourse to teleological considerations of costs and benefits to oneself, society, or any particular group.

As a basis or guide for ethical behavior, Kant's approach suggests that researchers should never treat their research participants as simply a means, but always as an end. This is not meant to imply that human beings should not be used for research purposes, but rather that they should never be treated as *mere* means, since they have worth independently of a researcher's need for them and should be treated accordingly.

By suggesting that the rightness of an action can be determined independently of consequences, the Kantian position encounters problems in application, particularly when rules conflict and exceptions to them must be made (Bunda, 1985). A version of the deontological approach that circumvents the latter problem has been developed by Ross (1930). Ross did not consider codes of behavior as rules, but as independently grounded obligations or duties, such as *beneficence* (duties requiring that the conditions of others be made better), *gratitude* (duties that result from services given by others), and *justice* (duties that result when benefits are not distributed in accordance with the merits of individuals). In situations where two or more duties are in conflict in a particular situation, Ross contended that what actually ought to be done is self-evident. This emphasizes the inexorability of moral conflict and the fact that duties are never absolute but rather *prima facie*, meaning that they are conditional on not being overridden by other moral principles. In other words, a *prima facie* duty is an obligation or a direct claim that lies on an individual as a result of the situation he or she faces.

According to Ross, in the abstract, the keeping of promises is always right as a rule of *prima facie* duty and exists as an obligation that one should try to fulfill. In actual practice, however, some other obligation or rule of *prima facie* duty that is held to have greater weight under the particular circumstances may intervene. The decision as to which duty outweighs the other is to be based on one's intelligence and reason. Since no rule of thumb can be given for all cases, a decision about which duty is stronger must be settled from case to case. Thus, while the keeping of one's promises, for example, must always be taken into account as a right-making consideration, other conflicting considerations may sometimes take precedence over it.

Unlike Kant, Ross showed how one can have a set of rules that do not have exceptions, by regarding them not as categorical imperatives but as rules of *prima facie* duty. Nevertheless, according to Frankena (1973), a limitation to Ross's duty-based, deontological theory lies in his claim that *prima facie* duties are self-evident. Ross did not believe that it was necessary to establish a criterion for determining what *prima facie* duties are and, in so doing, may have failed to establish clearly the determinants of what is morally right or wrong (Frankena, 1973).

Another nonutilitarian approach often associated with the deontological perspective describes principles of behavior in terms of individual rights rather than duties. Most clearly exhibited in the rights-based position of John Rawls (1971), the basic moral position is that rights and obligations are logically related. One person's right implies another's obligation to act in a way that benefits or protects the rights of the first person, and, in turn, obligations can imply rights. Various rights-based theories differ in terms of the rights they denote as either fundamental or derivative.

Rawls's (1971) position, sometimes referred to as the *justice as fairness* theory, evolved out of his dissatisfaction with the utilitarian approach, which allows for violations of the principle of justice. Utilitarians, for example, would probably approve a study expected to provide a cure for cancer, even though it would require the development of untreated cancer in some subjects. According to Rawls, such an example illustrates the failure of utilitarianism to account for the element of justice commonly conceived as fairness (Macklin & Sherwin, 1975). Although he agrees in principle that there is no reason why the violation of the rights of a few individuals might not be justified by the greater good shared by many—that is, that ethical considerations ought to account for general welfare—Rawls contends that ethical choices also must be concerned with justice.

Rawls formulated two principles of justice to serve as criteria for morally correct actions: (1) a justice system must have equality of liberty—that is, all persons have an equal right to the most extensive basic liberty compatible with a like liberty for all, and (2) social and economic inequalities are to be arranged so that they benefit the least advantaged the most, and that positions associated with such inequalities are open to everyone—that is, if inequalities are to exist, all must benefit from them. These principles of justice, according to Rawls, would be adopted by individuals if they were somehow constrained by a situation that rendered them all equal.

Applying these notions to the research context, it is clear that—as in the Kantian approach—certain studies would be rejected in principle regardless of their potential benefits. Studies that violate a liberty to which a person is entitled would be viewed as wrong, such as an experiment that might deprive its subjects of freedom of thought, or one that renders subjects unable to act as autonomous, independent beings. Studies designed to benefit persons other than the subjects also would not be approved if the subjects were already worse off than the intended beneficiaries. A study that involves an unequal distribution of risks can be justified by Rawls's position only if it benefits those individuals who are currently disadvantaged.

## Summary

In essence, teleological theories rely solely on the consequences of acts in judging the rightness or wrongness of the acts. The various teleological theories are distinguished by their answers to the specific questions, "What consequences are good consequences?" and "Consequences for whom?" (Atwell, 1981). As a teleological approach, utilitarianism focuses on the consequences of an action for the common good. Although deontological approaches consider consequences, they tend to focus instead on the relevant principles in a situation and consider moral behavior as an end in and of itself, rather than as a means to an end (Bunda, 1985). Of these approaches, it appears that Rawls's rights-based theory may be superior for evaluating applied social research because it draws on elements from other ethical approaches and sets forth principles for evaluating institutions and social arrangements where justice is a concern (Macklin & Sherwin, 1975; Reynolds, 1979). However, one must keep in mind that ultimately the acceptance of a moral theory is something each individual must do. When attempts are made to apply these ethical theories in practical matters, conflicts of interest and of fundamental principles among individuals are to be expected (Macklin & Sherwin, 1975; see Table 3.1).

## GOVERNMENTAL AND PROFESSIONAL STANDARDS

The ethical systems and structures to which social researchers now subscribe, largely by virtue of voluntary codes, governmental regulations, and professional standards, may be said to reflect community attitudes, professional experience, and technical standards. Having replaced the so-called unwritten professional ethic that presumed individuals would act in fair, considerate, and compassionate ways with regard to the rights of others, the current federal regulations and professional codes of ethics set forth ethical standards for guidance and control within social research disciplines. A summary of these controls and a brief historical perspective is presented below.

## Federal Regulations

In recent years the question of ethics in social research has been brought to the fore largely as a consequence of the increasing scope of U.S. governmental regulation, policies of the larger scientific community, and new research support requirements. As Sieber (1982a) has correctly noted, some of the political impetus for the regulation of human research came about as a result of widely publicized cases of ethical misuse and abuse of human participants in biomedical research.

In one of the first cases to achieve notoriety, two researchers working with federal funds during the early 1960s injected live cancer cells into 26 chronically ill patients receiving care from hospital staff at the Jewish Chronic Disease Hospital in Brooklyn, New York (Frankel, 1975). Some of the patients were told that something was going to be done to them of an experimental nature, but none was informed about the cancer cell injections, nor were they asked to give written consent for the procedure. The researchers expected that the ill patients would react to the foreign cells by rejecting them relatively quickly, as had healthy individuals. Although this result was obtained, both researchers subsequently were found guilty of fraud, deceit, and unprofessional conduct, and were censured and placed on a year's probation by the Board of Regents of the State University of New York (Faden & Beauchamp, 1986). This episode hardly destroyed the careers of the researchers; in fact, one was elected president of the American Association for Cancer Research in 1967. It did, however, raise the awareness of public agency officials about the actual and potential risks to human participants in clinical investigations. It also highlighted the uncertain legal position of government agencies and functioned as a significant precedent in the eventual development of federal guidelines (Faden & Beauchamp, 1986; Frankel, 1975).

A number of similar biomedical experiments—too numerous to describe here—have been conducted using humans without their informed consent (see Beecher, 1966; Pappworth, 1967; Veatch &

TABLE 3.1
## Summary of Moral Positions

| Philosophical School | Criteria for Action | Focus of Moral Decision |
|---|---|---|
| Teleological | | |
| Ethical Egoists (e.g., Nietzsche, Hobbes) | Well-being of moral agent | Consequences of alternative action |
| Utilitarians (e.g., J. S. Mill) | Aggregate common good | Consequences of alternative action |
| Deontological | | |
| Duty-Based (e.g., Kant, Ross) | Duties of behavior; e.g., fidelity, gratitude, justice | Relevant duties in the situation |
| Rights-Based (e.g., Rawls) | Rights of individuals; e.g., dignity, liberty | Relevant rights of individuals affected by actions |

SOURCE: Reprinted with permission from *Evaluation and Program Planning*, Vol. 8, M. Bunda, "Applied Alternative Systems of Ethics," copyright 1985, Pergamon Journals, Ltd.

Sollitto, 1973). Several of these studies are documented in psychiatrist Jay Katz's exhaustive anthology and casebook, *Experimentation With Human Beings*, published in 1972. The book, which draws from sociology, psychology, medicine, and law, traces the origins of political concern about the use of humans in research to the experiments conducted on prisoners in Nazi concentration camps during World War II, which led to the Nuremberg trials and eventual formulation of an international code of ethics to govern the conduct of medical research. The Nazi research included horrific experiments on healthy prisoners' reactions to various diseases (such as malaria, epidemic jaundice, and spotted fever), poisons, and simulated high altitudes; studies on the effectiveness of treatments for different types of experimentally induced wounds; and the measurement, execution, and defleshing of more than 100 persons for the purpose of completing a university skeleton collection (Katz, 1972).

Publication of Katz's anthology coincidentally came on the eve of public disclosures about the Tuskegee syphilis study, considered to be one of the most celebrated cases of research abuse in the United States and the longest nontherapeutic experiment on humans in medical history (Jones, 1981). The Tuskegee study was begun in 1932 by the U.S. Public Health Service to study the long-term effects of untreated syphilis in 399 semiliterate black men in Macon County, Alabama. Treatment purposely was withheld so that the "natural" course of the disease could be observed. An additional 201 black men without syphilis served as controls. The syphilitic subjects never were told about the true nature of their disease or that they were participants in a nontherapeutic experiment. Instead, they were informed that they were being treated for "bad blood," a term allegedly understood by the investigators to be a local euphemism for syphilis, but which the local blacks associated with unrelated ailments. Participation in the study was encouraged by the researchers' promises of "special free treatments," which included painful, nontherapeutic spinal taps.

It quickly became apparent that the infected subjects were suffering from more medical complications than the controls. By the mid-1940s, mortality rates were discovered to be twice as high for the untreated subjects; in fact, it was estimated that between 28-100 deaths as of 1969 were due to syphilis-related conditions. Nevertheless, the Public Health Service did not provide treatment for the disease until after the experiment was exposed in 1972 by Jean Heller, a *New York Times* reporter.

A panel appointed by the Department of Health, Education and Welfare (DHEW) to review the Tuskegee experiment concluded that established policies for reviewing experimental procedures and obtaining subjects' consent were virtually nonexistent in governmental agencies, and that more effective controls were needed to protect the rights of research participants. This assessment, in combination with increasing reports of other research controversies, apparently influenced Congress to appoint a national commission to examine both behavioral and biomedical research (Faden & Beauchamp, 1986). Established in July 1974 with the signing of the National Research Act, the National Commission for the Protection of Human Subjects of Biomedical and Behavioral Research was particularly instrumental in bringing delicate ethical issues to the attention of the public, researchers, and politicians. The National Commission provided recommendations to the secretary of DHEW to assure that behavioral and biomedical research comply with federal requirements.

The Department of Health and Human Services (DHHS, formerly DHEW) and one of its research funding agencies, the National Institutes of Health (NIH), have played an especially important role in governmental regulation of the use of human subjects in experimental areas. The current DHHS regulations, which appear in the January 26, 1981 issue of *Federal Register*, require that an institution funded in whole or in part by a Department grant, contract, or cooperative agreement, or fellowship for research involving human subjects provide for an institutional review board (IRB) to assure the protection and welfare of subjects.

In order to approve proposed research covered by the Department regulations, an IRB must determine whether the following conditions are met: (1) risks to subjects are minimized by sound research procedures that do not unnecessarily expose subjects to risks, (2) risks to subjects are outweighed sufficiently by anticipated benefits to the subjects and the importance of the knowledge to be gained, (3) the rights and welfare of subjects are adequately protected, (4) the activity will be periodically reviewed, and (5) informed consent has been obtained and appropriately documented.

As defined in the regulations, the basic elements of informed consent include: (1) an explanation of the procedures used in the experiment and their purposes, (2) a description of any reasonably foreseeable risks and discomforts to the subjects, (3) a description of any benefits that may reasonably be expected, (4) a disclosure of any alternative procedures that might be advantageous to the subject, (5) an offer to answer any questions concerning the procedures, and (6) a statement that participation is voluntary and that the subject is free to withdraw from participation at any time.

Prior to drafting and adoption of the current regulations, the thrust of previous DHHS regulatory policy was in the direction of greater mandatory IRB coverage of human subjects research (Seiler & Murtha, 1981). All research projects involving human participants conducted at or sponsored by grantee institutions were subject to review by an IRB whose governance and procedures were agency established. This meant that research receiving no direct federal funding was subject under regulation to IRB review if it was carried out in an institution that received support from DHHS for other research involving human subjects.

In drafting its current regulations, DHHS responded to recommendations of the National Commission, the President's Commission for the Study of Ethical Problems in Medicine and Biomedical and Behavioral Research, and public comment, breaking sharply with the trend established by earlier rules and recommendations. The new regulations apply directly only to research projects receiving agency funds and no longer apply to unfunded projects. Moreover, the regulations substantially reduce the scope of DHHS regulatory coverage by exempting broad categories of research that normally present little or no risk of harm to subjects (e.g., certain forms of research on educational strategies, techniques, and testing; survey and interview research; observational studies of public behavior; and research involving the collection or study of existing data bases, documents, and records). The regulations also specify that expedited review (an abbreviated procedure conducted by one IRB member, who is not empowered to veto a project) is appropriate for certain categories of minimal-risk research (e.g., research on teeth, hair, body wastes, and blood samples; voice recordings made for research purposes; research requiring moderate exercise by healthy volunteers; and nonmanipulative, stress-free studies of individual or group behavior or characteristics). This deregulation in federal policy has been interpreted as a prudent revision and conciliation by researchers who long maintained that the government, through DHHS, had overstepped its authority in attempting to regulate social research activities and that the former regulations (DHEW, 1974) needlessly interfered with risk-free investigations (McCarthy, 1981).

While unfunded studies conducted within research-oriented institutions such as universities and hospitals no longer require institutional review, it is generally assumed that investigators will apply professional ethical standards in conducting their research (Carroll et al., 1985). Professional standards, as described in the next section, typically place responsibility for ethical conduct on the individual researcher rather than on external enforcement. Prior to the National Commission recommendations, there was very little evidence of any type of committee review of research projects in university departments of medicine (Curran, 1969; Welt, 1961), and probably none at all in social and behavioral science areas (Reynolds, 1979). The widespread impact of the federal regulations is apparent in the results of a 1975 survey that reported the existence of at least 113 medical schools and 424 universities, research institutions, and organizations with institutional review boards (Institute for Social Research, 1976). Currently, it is likely that most universities and/or university departments are requiring some form of review for the approval and monitoring of unfunded research conducted by faculty and student researchers. However, there are legal and ethical questions pertaining to departmental reviews of their own proposals, including the possibility that the review will be biased in the direction of the department's own interests (Carroll et al., 1985). In addition, serious consequences can arise when university, state, and federal review procedures conflict (see, for example, Tedeschi & Rosenfeld, 1981).

## Summary

Present federal policy effectively removes the bulk of behavioral and social research from IRB scrutiny and shifts the burden of ethical responsibility to professional decision makers, individual researchers, and institution officials for generating reasonable and workable policies for non-DHHS and exempted DHHS research. The new federal regulations are to be regarded as a *minimum* of protections for human research participants; institutions are free to increase—but not reduce— the protections as they see fit (Faden & Beauchamp, 1986). Thus, in addition to federal regulations, investigators in the behavioral and social sciences have, by necessity, taken steps to provide standards for human research within their professional organizations.

## The Role of Professional
## Ethics in Social Research

Professional ethics activities reflect the willingness of a profession to self-regulate the behavior of its members on behalf of the public and the profession. In social research, *professional ethics* refers to the rules that define the rights and responsibilities of researchers in their relationships with each other and with other parties, including research subjects, clients, employers, and so on (Chalk, Frankel, & Chafer, 1980). A single set of ethical rules of conduct is not available for social researchers, who may work in a variety of scientific disciplines that have developed their own separate sets of standards for guiding and controlling human subject research.

The initial impetus for the development of professional codes for the responsible conduct of human experimentation came in the area of biomedical research. The best known of the codes developed to regulate biomedical research are the Nuremberg Code of 1947, the Helsinki Declaration of 1964 (revised in 1975), and the Draft Code of Ethics on Experimentation formulated by the World Medical Association in Geneva in 1961. The Nuremberg Code on research practices was established to prevent future atrocities such as those perpetrated under the guise of "medical science" by Nazi researchers. The 10-point code did not proscribe investigation as such, but attempted to outline permissible limits for experimentation. Most important, it brought to the fore the concept of "informed consent" for the first time.

During the 1960s, using these early codes as models, sociologists and anthropologists developed codes of research ethics in their respective fields. Following several years of study and debate, a code of ethics was adopted in 1969 by the American Sociological Association (ASA) and a standing committee on professional ethics was appointed. The 1969 code was revised in 1984 following concern that it emphasized research issues to the exclusion of other professional activities performed by sociologists. The 1984 version includes sections dealing with ethical rules related to research, publication and review processes, teaching and the rights of students, and relationships among sociologists. The current ASA code is representative of recent attempts by professional societies to address the ethical conflicts that occur at each of the levels associated with performing scientific research.

Position statements on problems of anthropological research and ethics first became available by the American Anthropological Association (AAA) in 1948, and were more fully articulated in 1967. A set of rules of professional responsibility was adopted by AAA in May 1971, building on the two earlier statements, and presently serves as the primary ethics statement of the Association and two other professional societies—the American Association of Physical Anthropologists and the American Ethnological Association. The current rules specify that the responsibilities of anthropologists extend to those individuals studied, the public, the discipline, students, sponsors, and one's own government and host governments. The rules also acknowledge that conflicts between the various responsibilities of anthropologists will occur and that choices between "conflicting values" will have to be made. Toward assisting anthropologists in addressing such conflicts, the rules emphasize that highest regard should be placed on the well-being of research subjects and the integrity of the profession, and that when these conditions cannot be followed, the research should not be conducted.

Affiliated societies and associations within other social science disciplines have engaged in similar ethical activities. For example, the first complete ethical code for human subject research in psychology was developed in 1973 by an ad hoc committee of the American Psychological Association (APA), although a more generic code detailing ethical considerations in research, teaching, and professional practices was available in 1953 (see below for further description of these codes). Several efforts also have been made recently to develop ethical standards for evaluation research (e.g., Evaluation Research Society, 1982; Joint Committee on Standards for Educational Evaluation, 1981). Brief summaries of the ethical activities in related social research disciplines, with excerpts from the various codes, are presented in Chalk et al.'s (1980) report on the Professional Ethics Project undertaken by the American Association for the Advancement of Science. In addition, Orlans (1973) and Dalglish (1976) provide detailed discussions of the development of ethical concern and ethical codes within social science professional associations.

The development of ethical standards for social researchers is interesting historically because of the process by which the standards were evolved and the changing political and social climate they reflected

(Reese & Fremouw, 1984). The early codes (e.g., APA, 1953; ASA, 1971) presented a few simple guidelines that were quite general and largely unenforceable, perhaps reflective of a period in which explicit concerns about social research seemed unnecessary (Sieber, 1982b). But the rise in social conscience and emphasis on the protection of individual rights ushered in during the late 1960s brought about a push for "relevant" research on urgent social problems, such as violence and crime, drug abuse, minority issues, and racial conflict. As the object of much social research changed, so too did the ethical guidelines established in the disciplines. Each revision of the ethical codes brought about more comprehensive guidelines that reflected more current social concerns.

The development of professional ethics in psychology provides an interesting case study in the evolution of guiding principles of conduct for social research. The beginnings of a code of ethics in psychology date back to 1938, when a special committee was formed to consider the advisability of drafting an ethical code. The committee concluded that any attempt to legislate a complete code would have been premature but recommended that a standing committee be appointed to consider complaints of unethical conduct. In 1947, the committee recommended that work begin on a formal code of ethics.

World War II accelerated demands for applied research, and the call for a code of ethics in psychology appears to have emerged, at least in part, as a result of increased emphasis on the problems of professional psychology. The war sensitized psychologists to the importance of ethics at a time when it was widely assumed that basic research was invariably ethical and value-free, and would eventually serve human welfare (Diener & Crandall, 1978). The formidable undertaking of developing a code was accomplished, for the most part, with the participation in 1948 of all members of APA, who were asked to describe actual situations in which they had to make decisions perceived as having ethical implications. Based on the ethically critical incidents described in the more than 1,000 responses received, a set of provisional standards was drafted and submitted to all APA members for review and comment. The formal code, *Ethical Standards of Psychologists*, was adopted in 1953 and has since undergone numerous revisions, most recently in January 1981.

By the late 1960s a changing scientific climate within psychology had begun to emerge, and with it came a great deal of uncertainty about the adequacy of *Ethical Standards* as it specifically applied to the use of human subjects in research. Characteristics of this changing climate, such as the growing scale of psychological research with human subjects and the special ethical problems that accompanied emerging areas of research, appear to have contributed to an increased concern among psychologists about the ethics of their methods. Despite the early progress on ethics in psychology, it was not until publication of and ensuing debate over some highly controversial studies that psychologists seriously began to wrestle with the issues of deception, privacy, and confidentiality in human subject research.

One of the first landmark cases of controversial social research has come to be known as the Wichita Jury Study. Begun in 1954 by a group of professors at the University of Chicago Law School, the study raised serious questions about confidentiality and privacy in social research (Vaughan, 1967). Although the study was conducted by nonpsychologists, its method and subject matter hit very close to home for psychologists, and it quickly made its way into the psychology literature. The researchers, in their attempt to study the adequacy of the jury decision-making process, used hidden microphones to record secretly the jury deliberations of six separate civil cases. These recordings were made with the knowledge and prior approval of opposing counsel and the judges involved in the cases, but the jurors, defendants, and plaintiffs were not informed about any aspect of the research. It was agreed beforehand that the recordings would not be listened to until after the cases had been closed and all appeals exhausted, and that transcripts of the deliberations would be edited to ensure the anonymity of all participants involved.

The Wichita Jury Study quickly generated a national uproar when it was made public by a cooperating trial judge who played one of the tape recordings to a judicial committee (Faden & Beauchamp, 1986). This revelation resulted in a congressional hearing and, ultimately, legislation that prohibited intrusions upon the privacy of juries (including the tape recording of their deliberations). Public criticism of the research centered on the methods used to collect the information, emphasizing that secret jury deliberations are essential to the American judicial system as guaranteed by the Seventh Amendment to the Constitution. Others argued that to the extent that the jurors were unaware that they were being recorded, their rights to autonomy and privacy had been violated. Another issue raised was the possibility that general knowledge about the project could reduce the degree of openness and candor in subsequent juries.

In defending their research, the investigators focused on the potential benefits of the study, claiming that its successful completion would have either boosted confidence in the current jury system or else suggested recommendations for positive change in the judicial decision-making process. They also answered that their findings could have been used to assess the extent to which mock juries in other studies simulated the behavior of actual juries.

The Wichita Jury Study came to the attention of psychologists largely as a result of an article that appeared in the *American Psychologist* in 1966. Its authors, Ruebhausen and Brim, discussed the study as an example of the invasion of privacy in behavioral research, and recommended that psychology adopt a set of ethical standards that make explicit the researcher's obligation to obtain informed consent in order to protect their subjects' right to privacy.

Concern among psychologists about the ethicality of the Wichita Jury Study, while considerable, was nothing compared to the controversy that emerged following publication of a series of behavioral studies of obedience conducted between 1960-1964 by Stanley Milgram, a social psychologist at Yale University. Milgram's experiments involved an elaborate deception that led subjects to believe that they were giving dangerous electric shocks to an innocent victim. Briefly, Milgram recruited volunteers to participate in an experiment allegedly on the effects of punishment on learning. Subjects were placed in the role of teachers who were assigned the task of teaching a list of words to a learner (actually an experimental confederate). The procedure required subjects to "punish" the learner's mistakes by delivering increasingly stronger electric shocks (up to 450 volts). The experiment was rigged so that the learner would not actually receive shocks, but would make a number of preplanned mistakes and feign pain upon receiving the "shocks." The true aim of the study was to observe the extent to which subjects obeyed the authority of the experimenter, who commanded that subjects proceed with the procedure despite their protests and the confederate's apparent agony. The high degree of obedience obtained in the experiments was unsettling in that it demonstrated the extent to which ordinary citizens might engage in brutal behavior at the direction of a malevolent authority.

Critical reactions to the obedience studies were voiced almost immediately upon publication of Milgram's initial reports of his findings, beginning in 1963. (The lay public first learned of the research in 1974 when Milgram's book, *Obedience to Authority*, was published.) Critics argued that there were not adequate measures taken to protect the participants; that the entire program of experiments should have been terminated as soon as it was observed that they were causing undue stress on the participants; and that the participants would in the future be alienated from psychological research because of the intensity of experience associated with laboratory procedures (see Baumrind, 1964; Kelman, 1967).

Milgram (1964) countered these arguments by asserting that adequate measures *were* taken to protect the participants, all of whom were allowed to abandon the experiment at any time, and at the end of the experiment were thoroughly debriefed and shown that the "victim" had not actually received the electric shocks. He also maintained that the experiments should *not* have been terminated, because there was no indication of injurious effects in the subjects; indeed, the subjects themselves later endorsed the experiment in a follow-up questionnaire and indicated that they were not alienated from psychological research.

Milgram further answered his critics by suggesting that the perception of the ethicality of his use of deception may revolve around the results he obtained. Support for this contention was obtained by Bickman and Zarantonello (1978), who presented adult subjects with four versions of Milgram's experimental design, in which both the degree of obedience and the amount of deception were varied in the description presented. Those subjects who read the version indicating that a high level of obedience had resulted rated the design as potentially more harmful than those who read versions indicating that a low level of obedience had resulted. In other words, their perceptions of the study were more contingent upon the outcome of the experiments than upon the particular deception procedures used to obtain the results. Thus Milgram's experiments might have generated far less condemnation if his results had turned out differently. Of course, from a duty-based deontological perspective such as Kant's, the Milgram studies would be viewed as immoral regardless of the degree of obedience that resulted. According to the Kantian argument, it was "categorically wrong" for Milgram to have deceived his subjects (Rosnow, 1981).

While the above examples of social research do not begin to approach the seriousness of the known abuses that have occurred in biomedical experimentation, studies such as the Wichita Jury Study, Milgram's obedience experiments, Humphreys's "tearoom trade" research (described in Chapter 1), and other leading cases that have not been discussed here (such as Zimbardo's 1971 prison study) added to the climate of increased ethical sensitivities within psychology. At a time when psychology was suffering from growing pains, a reevaluation of its ethics surely was in order. Consequently, a method patterned after that used to develop the more generic code (*Ethical Standards*) led to development of the 1973 *Research Principles*, which dealt solely with the use of humans as research participants.

The *Research Principles*, revised for the first time in 1982, contains 10 general ethical statements in seven areas of concern: (1) making the decision to conduct a given investigation, (2) obtaining subjects' informed consent to participate, (3) assuring freedom from coercion to participate, (4) maintaining fairness in the research relationship, (5) protecting subjects from physical and mental harm, (6) observing responsibilities to participants once the research is completed, and (7) guaranteeing anonymity of research participants and confidentiality of data. Throughout the *Research Principles* and *Ethical Standards* an emphasis is placed on the researcher's personal responsibility for ethical decision making.

## Summary

The process by which psychology's first ethical documents were developed may have been as significant a means of encouraging high standards as the products themselves (Golann, 1970). A code developed on the basis of incidents actually faced by members of the profession may be less vulnerable to the often-voiced criticism that professional codes of ethics provide general guidance but few specific answers to the individual confronted with a dilemma. Each attempt at revision of the ethical guidelines in psychology has been similarly participatory and responsive to current demands (Reese & Fremouw, 1984). For example, sexual harassment is explicitly defined and prohibited by the current standards, although this ethical issue was not addressed in the APA guidelines prior to 1981.

## Professional Ethics and
## Governmental Regulation

Ethical activities in psychology and related disciplines are a response to continued concern that the potential impact of research on human participants and society should not be ignored in the pursuit and subsequent application of knowledge. However, professional codes of ethics serve somewhat different functions than do governmental regulations (Lowman & Soule, 1981). Federal and state laws require scientists to take certain precautions or forbid them from engaging in certain activities likely to increase the risk of harm to an individual or to society. Governmental regulations are designed to protect or advance the interests of society and individuals who make up that society, and the mechanism by which they are enforced is the established system of law in the society.

Professional codes of ethics, while sharing the goal of laws and regulations to protect society and its individual members from harm, exist primarily to instruct members of the profession in behaviors considered appropriate by their peers. Ethical standards are enforced by members of the profession as a means of socializing those entering the profession to the acceptable behaviors related to questions of morality, professional judgment, technique, or simply good professional manners. In every decision-making situation, the professional is armed with the ethical maxims of his or her scientific community, but these standards serve as "illuminators" or exemplars of the ethical problem at hand. Whereas governmental regulations are to be adhered to as directives, an ethical decision may or may not be consistent with the standards of the profession. The ethical standards for social researchers are a set of normative rules. The professional is free to exercise judgment regarding research procedures, allowing for exceptions to the ethical standards of the profession if they seem justified by the uniqueness of the situation (Lowman & Soule, 1981). Consistent with this role, and while providing some assurance that recognized requirements will be met and sensitivities to the issues sharpened, professional codes of ethics in social research are not guarantees for the full protection of research participants, society, and scientific integrity, but might instead be regarded as "stop-and-go signals with mechanisms for movement" for those who conduct research (Ladimer, 1970, p. 565).

Some individuals have criticized the cost-benefit approach implicit in most professional codes of ethics for social research, arguing that clearly formulated principles tend to be established along with a parallel system of rationalizations that condone, and may serve to encourage, conduct in violation of the principles (e.g., Baumrind, 1975; Bok, 1978). Typical of these arguments, Baumrind (1975) objected to the use of cost-benefit analyses for resolving ethical conflicts, claiming that such an approach inevitably leads to subjective decision making and moral dilemmas. Since, in Baumrind's view, the function of a system of moral philosophy is precisely to avoid such dilemmas, she attacked professional codes of ethics for failing to set forth clearly what is right or wrong in order to provide the researcher with guidance in dealing with specific ethical questions.

In response to critics such as Baumrind, it can be noted that a set of ethical principles or rules of conduct is only one important part of the overall machinery needed to effect self-regulation in social research. When one considers the great variety in human judgments regarding difficult ethical issues, it becomes unreasonable to expect an enforceable ethical code to emerge that can be considered absolute. Professional ethics committees typically are forced to recognize that reasonable people need not agree in their solutions to ethical problems.

## SUMMARY

It is probably safe to assume that the current guidelines for social science provide at least a workable framework within which individual researchers who seek guidance can analyze the issues relevant to the demands of their research. But without appropriate governmental and public policy activities to encourage proper professional conduct, and the means to detect and investigate possible violations and impose sanctions for wrongdoing, the impact of professional standards on its members may be negligible (Chalk et al., 1980).

## RECOMMENDED READINGS

Beauchamp, T. L. (1982). *Philosophical ethics*. New York: McGraw-Hill.
Beecher, H. K. (1970). *Research and the individual: Human studies*. Boston: Little, Brown.
Center for the Study of Ethics in the Professions. (1981). *Compilation of statements relating to standards of professional responsibility and freedom*. Chicago: Author.
Chalk, R., Frankel, M. S., & Chafer, S. B. (1980). *AAAS Professional Ethics Project: Professional ethics activities in the scientific and engineering societies*. Washington, DC: American Association for the Advancement of Science.
Frankena, W. K. (1973). *Ethics* (2nd ed.). Englewood Cliffs, NJ: Prentice-Hall.
Rawls, J. (1971). *A theory of justice*. Cambridge, MA: Harvard University Press.
Sieber, J. E. (1980). Being ethical: Professional and personal decisions in program evaluation. In R. Perloff & E. Perloff (Eds.), Values, ethics, and standards [Special issue]. *New Directions for Program Evaluation, 7*, 51-63.
Zimbardo, P. G. (1974). On the ethics of intervention in human psychological research: With special reference to the Stanford prison experiment. *Cognition, 2*, 243-256.

## CHAPTER EXERCISES

1. *Case Study:* An experiment has been proposed as an attempt to help in the understanding, and eventual curing, of depression. It will require the stimulation of a few initial subjects' brains with electrodes in order to produce in them a permanent, incapacitating state of depression that will be carefully studied until their deaths. Assuming that the researchers are convinced the experiment will be useful, (1) How would you expect a utilitarian, a duty-based (Kantian) theorist, and a rights-based theorist to respond to the research proposal? (2) What

conditions would the researchers have to satisfy in order to have their study approved (if at all) by the Department of Health and Human Services and the American Psychological Association?

2. Assume the role of John Stuart Mill, Immanuel Kant, or John Rawls, and write a short essay that reflects the views of the philosopher on the use of deception in human subject research. (Note: In order to assume the role effectively it will be necessary for you to read one or two original essays by these philosophers. Edited books of readings on ethical theory, such as Frankena and Granrose [1974] and Pahel and Schiller [1970] will be useful in this regard.)

# 4

# Methodological Issues
# and Dilemmas

This chapter provides a critical analysis of the conflicts between the practical (scientific) and ethical imperatives of applied social research, and assesses the impact of existing mechanisms on research methodology. There has been some recent concern among social and behavioral scientists (e.g., Adair, Dushenko, & Lindsay, 1985; Baumrind, 1985) that compliance with ethical procedures designed to protect the rights of human subjects poses certain methodological problems and may, in fact, have a substantial impact on experimental results. These problems are likely to be exacerbated by the basic nature and goals of applied social research, and special care must be taken to prevent the occurrence of unanticipated research effects that might emerge in this context.

Taken together, the general ethical requirements for applied social research are not different in nature from those that guide basic research. Regardless of the ultimate goals of a proposed investigation, ethical mechanisms require sensitivity to all aspects of scientific activity that engender ethical concerns, including formulation of the research question and design, conduct of the research and treatment of participants, consideration of the institutional context in which the research is conducted, and interpretation and application of research findings (Sieber & Stanley, 1988). However, applied social research investigations are distinct from most other studies in controlled settings and natural contexts in that they tend to deal with significant aspects of the psychological, behavioral, and social functioning of individual participants, and often involve interventions—hypothesized to have beneficial effects on a particular aggregate of individuals—in an ongoing social, economic, or organizational unit of society. *Social interventions* are best defined as "deliberate attempts by professionals to change the characteristics of individuals or groups, or to influence the pattern of relationships between individuals and/or groups" (Kelman & Warwick, 1978, p. 4). Much of the research in this area consists of attempts at planned change directed at such efforts as organizational development or community action programs. Other areas of application of intervention studies have involved treatments for lower-class minority groups, such as the prevention intervention approach described in Chapter 1. Individuals stand to benefit from their participation in the research, and, as such, the ethical problems encountered might be viewed as falling within the general set of ethical considerations involved in therapeutic innovations (Moore, 1970).

The protection of subjects' rights to informed consent and freedom from coercion to participate in research, and constraints upon the undue use of deception and concealment, are ethical requirements likely to present the social researcher with important methodological considerations. In turn, the methodological requirements of random selection and assignment of participants to experimental conditions in more controlled studies raise additional ethical issues, such as those involving the use of volunteer subject groups, the appropriateness of including untreated controls in intervention studies, and the potentially negative effects of early identification of research participants.

## INFORMED CONSENT AND SOCIAL RESEARCH

Voluntary informed consent is considered by many as the central norm governing the relationship between the investigator and the research participant. In this view, ethical problems generally arise when this norm is violated or circumvented, as the biomedical, jury, and obedience studies discussed in Chapter 3 clearly demonstrated. Perhaps the most cogent criticism of informed consent is that it is, in many cases, much too easy a hurdle for the investigator to clear. Recent surveys in psychology, for example, have revealed that the proportion of studies that reported obtaining informed consent or explicitly giving subjects the freedom to withdraw was negligible, and that the frequency and intensity of deception have not been reduced by ethical regulations (Adair et al., 1985; Baumrind, 1985). The informed consent requirement in existing ethical codes and guidelines permits the investigator to violate premises of the explicit contractual agreement with his or her subjects, which no doubt can be expected to lead to a loss of confidence in the investigator's integrity. For example, a qualification to the informed consent guideline in APA's *Research Principles* states that the "methodological requirements of a study may make the use of concealment or deception necessary," and that failure to obtain completely informed consent "requires additional safeguards" (APA, 1982, p. 6).

Originally developed for biomedical research, the informed consent procedure tends to be less readily applicable in social research, since it is often difficult to identify the degree of risk involved (which, for the most part, is less dramatic than for biomedical studies) and the extent to which subjects are truly informed (Adair et al., 1985). As a function of the power differential between the researcher and the subject in the context of a consent decision, subjects who voluntarily come to an investigation are confident that the researcher will respect their welfare (Baumrind, 1985; Epstein, Suedfeld, & Silverstein, 1973; Holder, 1982). In general, people want to trust the scientist-expert, and are naturally influenced by his or her persuasiveness and conviction. Thus, although consent may carry with it the notion of freedom, a person may be informed about an experiment and agree to it, but may have chosen to participate under subtle coercion. This problem is especially apparent in university settings where experimental participation is one way partially to fulfill course requirements.

While the importance of informed consent goes unquestioned, there are scientific considerations that override the practical and moral reasons for open and honest disclosure with potential participants, and controversy prevails over the nature and possibility of truly informed consent. It is generally understood that the concept of informed consent is neither in practice nor in law a single, clearly defined entity, but elusive and complex, whether viewed psychologically, philosophically, or morally (Jaffe, 1969; Katz, 1972; Levine, 1975a). The complexity arises, in part, from a futile attempt to define it in a way that is equally valid for every research situation. For example, it has been noted that the principle that underlies consent is that the subject must have enough information about the investigator and the research to form the basis for reasonable trust (Jaffe, 1969). But the operational definition of informed consent remains in an area of judgment, since a decision has to be made by each individual investigator about what constitutes, under varying circumstances, consent that is sufficiently informed.

### The Issue of Sufficient Information

Most codes of research ethics establish specific criteria for disclosure to assure that subjects are sufficiently informed. These generally include: (1) a statement to the subject indicating that participation is voluntary; (2) a description of what the subject can expect in terms of the essential methods of the research, the purposes of the methods, possible risks and anticipated benefits, and alternative procedures; and (3) a statement offering the subject the opportunity to ask questions and the freedom to withdraw at any time. Additional elements may be divulged, including an explanation of how and why the subject was selected, and information about the individual(s) most responsible for the research, the sponsorship of the research, and the possible uses to which the data or conclusions might be put.

Unfortunately, a simple itemization does not provide the researcher with much guidance for judging how much and what sort of information should be communicated to subjects in specific situations. Taken literally, "fully informed consent" is unattainable in most research situations. In addition to the fact that it would require the researcher to explain endless technical details to each participant, often the researcher does not know all of the answers pertinent to the research. For most social research, the full disclosure of every item listed for consent is unnecessary. Levine (1975a, p. 72) presented a long list of the types of information that could be included for fully informed consent, but added:

> In most cases most of these factors and devices will be found inappropriate or unnecessary. Each negotiation for informed consent must be adjusted to meet the requirements of the specific proposed activity and, more particularly, be sufficiently flexible to meet the needs of the individual prospective subject.

Similarly, the American Psychological Association (1982, p. 36) advises that the scope of any research project necessitates that informed consent need only be comprehensive to the extent that the investigator believes reasonably might influence willingness to participate in the research:

> Providing complete information about all of the considerations that might be important to potential participants is obviously impracticable and unacceptable to the research participant and the investigator alike. It is often desirable, however, for the investigator to double-check his or her judgment in this respect by consulting with qualified others and by responding fully to the potential participants' questions about the research.

Informed consent becomes especially important in social intervention programs, primarily because individuals may be strongly and/or immediately influenced by the research, much more so than is typical in purely theoretical investigations. When subjects may be permanently changed by an experiment, the importance of voluntary participation is magnified. Special care must be taken to inform potential subjects about their rights and obligations, the procedures they will undergo, potential risks and anticipated benefits, and their freedom to withdraw at any time. When studying minority group members, children, and non-English-speaking groups, certain difficulties arise from their differential status, including limited possibilities of articulation and understanding to judge adequately the purpose, risks, and other aspects of the investigation. These limitations further threaten the adequacy of the informed consent process, and increase the danger of subtly, perhaps unintentionally, coercing relatively powerless individuals into social research.

## Assessing the Adequacy
## of Informed Consent

The process of informed consent apparently is modulated by the probability and degree of risk to participants (Jaffe, 1969). Surely, the procedure for obtaining consent must be increasingly thorough as the possibility of danger and potential costs to participants and society become more likely, or as participants' rights are relinquished. Ladimer's (1970, p. 585) suggestion that the information provided to subjects must be "suited to individual differences in intellect, emotional status, and competence in decision making" reveals an additional consideration. Concern about how consent is to be gained when an aspect of the investigation or relevant technical information is too complex for a subject's immediate understanding and evaluation puts an added responsibility on the investigator to ensure adequate comprehension at the individual level. If a potential subject cannot grasp the entire situation, consent would be illusory (Edsall, 1969). The investigator, therefore, must adapt the presentation of information to each subject's intellectual capacity and then ascertain the degree of comprehension.

Consent forms that require an individual to restate in writing what he or she has agreed to should be useful for ascertaining comprehension of other aspects of the research (such as costs, benefits, and right to freely withdraw). Miller and Willner (1974) have developed a "two-part consent form" for research projects in which there is a large amount of complex information presented to the prospective subject. The two-part form consists of a standard consent form followed by a brief quiz on the essential elements of information that have already been presented.

Brown (1975) has proposed that the reliability of informed consent in protecting the rights of participants varies, depending on two factors that must be considered simultaneously: (1) the extent to which subjects possess information needed for rational deliberation (ranging from full capability for rational deliberation to impaired deliberative capability), and (2) the extent to which they are placed at risk or have their privacy threatened (ranging from no risk and complete privacy to substantial risk and impaired or threatened privacy). Within this framework, the more an experiment involves risks and the less subjects are freely able to give their informed consent (e.g., due to barriers to rational decision making or failures of communication and comprehension), the less the concerns of the consent process will be satisfied. Such problematic cases might be corrected through changes in experimental design (to reduce risks) and through education or careful presentation of information (to improve rational deliberation). Informed consent may not be required in situations where risks and invasions of privacy are unlikely, as in most simple observations of public behavior that do not lead to identification of those observed or cause them harm (e.g., research on crowd behavior).

Another recommendation offered by Brown is that the investigator should rely on the principle of *inverse selection* when a study threatens to expose subjects to harm. In short, the principle of inverse selection suggests that individuals vary along a continuum according to their ability truly to consent, and that the investigator should select a subject sample from among persons most able to consent. Ability to consent may be limited by lack of practice in making decisions, lack of education, information inaccurately conveyed or difficult to understand, difficulty in articulating lifetime objectives, and difficulty in rationing between present and future consumption (Brown, 1975). As a standard for the ethical selection of subjects, inverse selection is the opposite of a social utility standard that holds that the first candidates for risk and sacrifice should be drawn from the most available and expendable segments of society.

A drawback to inverse selection is that subject samples likely will be nonrepresentative; consequently, generalizations drawn exclusively from the use of such samples will be biased. In the past, informed consent guidelines have been questioned on the grounds that, once implemented, participants cease to represent a cross-section of the population and become instead a self-selected group (Zeisel, 1970). Inverse selection would exacerbate the threat to representativeness to the degree that differentiating characteristics between individuals who are able to consent and those unable to consent jeopardize the robustness of research conclusions derived solely from samples of subjects most able to consent. Although the utility of inverse selection may be somewhat limited in practice, Brown's avocation of the principle as a heuristic device to sensitize researchers to the characteristics of persons most able to understand consent fully bears some merit.

## The Impact of Informed
## Consent on Research Practice

A special problem of consent arises when the disclosure of pertinent aspects of a study raises the possibility that the research results will be deceptive or misleading. As described in Chapter 2, an informed consent dilemma emerges when methodological requirements of a study demand that participants remain unaware of information regarding their participation in a study or the specific hypotheses under investigation. The dilemma is posed by the likelihood that valid data could not be obtained if participants were fully informed of the purposes and procedures of the research (APA, 1982).

There are individuals who believe that strict adherence to the letter of the law requiring researchers first to obtain voluntary informed consent from their subjects is likely to interfere with even the best research design, and will destroy the possibility of doing needed social research. Recent studies that specifically introduced informed consent guidelines as a manipulated variable demonstrate that these fears are, to some extent, justified.

*Effects of informed consent on laboratory research.* Informing subjects about the purpose and procedures of a study has been found to alter subjects' data by reducing the spontaneity and naivete in their responses to manipulated variables in a controlled setting. Gardner (1978) conducted an experiment to test the effects of federal informed consent regulations on the results of environmental noise research. In brief, his study focused on negative performance aftereffects of noise by comparing a group of subjects that gave informed consent with a group that had not. The findings revealed that only subjects from whom informed consent was obtained failed to show the expected negative performance aftereffects. Gardner concluded, in part, that the consent form, with its references to subjects' freedom to withdraw from an experiment without penalty, may have contributed to informed subjects' perceived control over the noise.

Other studies (e.g., Dill, Gilden, Hill, & Hanselka, 1982; Resnick & Schwartz, 1973; Robinson & Greenberg, 1980) have similarly demonstrated that the informed consent procedure, including the explicit permission to withdraw, can seriously alter research results obtained in laboratory experiments, even without the disclosure of hypothesis-related information to subjects.

*Effects of informed consent on social survey research.* Since most applied social research investigations are conducted in natural settings, the impact of informed consent may be a less serious problem than in the laboratory setting. Research on the impact of informed consent in nonlaboratory research primarily has focused on its effects on the rate and quality of response in social survey research. Unlike the situation in the laboratory setting, the power differential between the investigator and the potential respondent is somewhat reversed in survey research, with the respondent typically in a powerful position to refuse to participate (Sieber, 1982a). Thus the key issue may not be informed consent, but rather privacy and confidentiality (the focus of Chapter 5).

In one study, Singer (1978) considered the effects on overall rate of response, response rates to individual questions, and response quality of factors that constitute informed consent in face-to-face survey interviews dealing with generally sensitive topics. Her findings revealed that more detailed, informative, and truthful information provided to potential respondents ahead of time about the content of the survey (i.e., disclosure of the sensitive content of questions) affected neither overall response rate nor responses to specific survey questions. The request for and timing of a signature to document consent affected both overall response rate and quality of response. Higher response rates were obtained from participants not asked for a signature than from those asked to sign before or after the interview. Asking subjects to sign the consent form before the interview apparently had a sensitization effect, with respondents more likely to report less socially undesirable behavior than respondents asked to sign a consent form afterwards.

In a follow-up study, Singer and Frankel (1982) varied information about the content and purpose of telephone, rather than face-to-face, interviews. While neither manipulated consent variable significantly affected overall response rate, response to individual items, or quality of response, the highest response rate and fewest refusals were obtained when potential respondents were provided with the greatest detail about the contents and purpose of the interview. Loo (1982) similarly reported a high level of cooperation among respondents who were given an opportunity to vent serious concerns to respectful and sympathetic investigators.

Overall, these studies suggest that the averse impact of informed consent on social survey research is negligible. With the exception of request for a signature to document consent (a procedure that typically is unnecessary, so long as respondents are afforded the right to refuse to respond to the interview or specified questions within it), the elements of informed consent do not appear to have much of an effect on response rates or quality of responses to social surveys. Nonetheless, this conclusion should be viewed with caution prior to further investigation of the mediating variables that are operative in different consent situations. There is some evidence, for example, that subjects may not fully attend to what they are told during the consent procedure, thus questioning the extent to which truly informed consent had been obtained in studies such as those described above (Singer, 1978). Other research has shown that informed consent can reduce participation and response to specific items in surveys (Lueptow, Mueller, Hammes, & Master, 1977). Finally, it should be noted that the content and purpose of a survey may interact with various response variables. Informed consent might be expected to reduce participation and item response rates for specific questions for welfare clients (asked about income), employees in large corporations (asked about their drinking habits), and so on (Singer, 1978).

*Solutions to the informed consent dilemma.* Toward a solution to the dilemma of informed consent and research validity, care should be taken to distinguish cases in which disclosure would invalidate the research from cases in which disclosure would not threaten empirical results and subsequent causal inference. In most situations, omitting the purpose of the study from the informed consent procedure will not present an ethical problem provided that participants are informed of all possible risks that can be reasonably anticipated by the investigators. In other situations, it may be unclear whether informed consent is mandatory. For these cases, the investigator may want to determine prior to actual research whether potential subjects would agree to participate in the study if all aspects of the research were made known to them.

Several strategies are available for assessing the need for informed consent prior to conducting the research. The most common strategy, in lieu of actually obtaining this information from subjects, is for the investigator simply to estimate whether potential subjects would consent once informed (Berscheid et al., 1973). Baumrind (1971) has advised that, for an experiment to be run without informed consent, no more than 5 out of 100 pretested subjects should express dissatisfaction with the experimental procedure. Another way to obtain information on the necessity for informed consent involves a role-play sampling procedure referred to as "anticipated consent" (Berscheid et al., 1973). *Anticipated consent* is the procedure by which persons drawn from the subject population are asked to role play a proposed experimental procedure and to estimate how they would feel if they were actual participants.

Researchers often attempt to protect the validity of their research by relying on what might be called "misinformed consent," when they consider it necessary purposely to mislead or misinform their subjects (Diener & Crandall, 1978). Whether or not such active deceptions (and subsequent debriefings) are successful in circumventing the problems of validity is, as yet, an unresolved issue (Adair et al., 1985; Diener & Crandall, 1978). Active deceptions are usually quite different from omissions of pertinent information, and the practice of deception in social research has aroused considerable debate on both ethical and methodological questions (e.g., Baumrind, 1964, 1985; Bok, 1978; Kelman, 1967). Ethical codes have placed restrictions on the use of deception in research, but do not rule out the necessity of its use in light of the methodological requirements of a study. For example, the 1982 APA code maintains that prior to conducting a study, the investigator has a

> special responsibility to (1) determine whether the use of such techniques is justified by the study's prospective scientific, educational, or applied value; (2) determine whether alternative procedures are available that do not use concealment or deception; and (3) ensure that the participants are provided with sufficient explanations as soon as possible. (American Psychological Association, 1982, p. 6)

In essence, the solution to the use of deception in social research requires the investigator to weigh the costs and benefits for each study, explore alternative research strategies, and to employ debriefing in cases where deception is used. Difficulties inherent in cost-benefit analyses are discussed in subsequent chapters. The debriefing process, which increasingly has become a standard part of the procedure in laboratory research, would require a researcher who has deceived his or her subjects to explain to them the true nature of the experiment, apologize for the deception, and, if possible, provide feedback of the results. As such, debriefing could provide subjects with a view that they are gullible or naive, which in turn might lower their self-esteem and undermine their trust in the scientific endeavor (Kelman, 1972). These subjects might become less compliant in future research because of their feelings about being "taken in." In addition, research has demonstrated that routine debriefing can produce widespread suspicion among populations frequently tapped for subjects (Brock & Becker, 1966; Stricker, Messick, & Jackson, 1967).

## Summary

Few researchers feel that we can do entirely without deception, since the adoption of an overly conservative approach could deem the study of important research areas hardly worthy of the effort. For instance, a study of racial prejudice accurately labeled as such would certainly affect subjects' behavior. Deception studies differ so greatly in the nature and degree of deception that even the harshest critic would be hard pressed to state unequivocally that all deception has potentially harmful effects or is otherwise wrong.

The decision to deceive research subjects actively ultimately depends heavily upon the investigator's resolution of the complex issues relating to informed consent and the balancing of costs and benefits. The effects of deception on the autonomy of one's subjects always need to be considered, in terms of the extent to which they compromise subjects' ability to understand fully that to which they are giving their consent (Faden & Beauchamp, 1986). Nevertheless, for some moral philosophers, deception is always wrong-making (e.g., in Ross's view it is a *prima facie* wrong) and, therefore, always requires a justification. The problem inherent in leaving the justification of deceptive methods to researchers' judgments is that this readily permits excessive rationalizations in the service of the decision makers' self-interest. One need only be reminded of the blatant deceptions implemented in the Tuskegee study, where subjects consented to painful spinal taps after being falsely informed that they would be receiving a "special free treatment," to recognize the potential dangers of leaving researchers free to decide whether deceptions is necessary.

When researchers learn as part of their training to solve methodological problems through the practice of deception, there is always the possibility that deception later will be used as a matter of course (Kelman, 1967; Murray, 1980). Deception that is used more out of laziness or habit than out of methodological necessity can never be morally justified. A more promising program for professional conduct would be one that considers deception only as a last resort. Thus it is essential that researchers continue to search for, develop, and implement alternatives to deception that would be welcomed by their subjects.

## ETHICAL ISSUES IN THE SELECTION AND ASSIGNMENT OF RESEARCH PARTICIPANTS

Many of the social intervention studies now being undertaken (such as those in the area of prevention research) involve random assignment of treatment and no-treatment (or other contrast) conditions to experimental and control participants. In selecting and assigning research participants in these experiments, researchers might be confronted by ethical problems relevant to the use of volunteer subjects and untreated control groups. In large part, these problems emerge when, for various practical reasons, the methodological requirements of random selection and random assignment of participants cannot be satisfied. In short, *random selection* means that all persons in the population being studied have an equal chance of being selected to participate in the study. By *random assignment* it is meant that every subject has an equal chance of being assigned to any of the study's treatment conditions.

### The Volunteer Problem

As a proposed solution to the danger of coercing individuals from among the most powerless groups in society into programs that researchers consider to be beneficial to them, voluntary social research programs raise an additional set of ethical issues. Foremost among these issues is the possibility that researchers will make promises in their recruitment efforts that cannot be carried out. For example, in the area of preventive intervention research, controlled studies actually demonstrating that intervention techniques have a preventive effect are not widely available. Thus a researcher's confidence in the effectiveness of a particular technique in preventing mental health problems might promote behavior that approaches a kind of "false advertising." False hopes may be created among volunteers, thereby unjustifiably raising their expectations about the potential benefits of participation.

One means to circumvent the problem of raising false hopes is for researchers to communicate to potential subjects the belief that a study has a reasonable chance of positive effects, and little chance of damaging effects, while taking care not to oversell the potential benefits of the approach. For example, in testing the utility of interventions for the prevention of depression, Muñoz (1983) tells potential participants that the methods have been found helpful in controlling depression that interferes with daily functioning, but that the techniques first must be learned by participants and will not necessarily work for all people in all situations. In this way, Muñoz conveys the message that research involvement *may* be beneficial to the individual, but that even after successfully learning the prevention techniques, there is no guarantee that they can be successfully applied to prevent depression.

Another issue encountered by decisions to limit social programs solely to volunteers is that programs could subtly work to exclude from participation individuals from certain societal or ethnic groups, without necessarily being overtly discriminatory. For example, Muñoz (1983) has argued that in our well-intended attempts not to coerce people into our research programs, we may be withholding valuable resources from those most in need. This process could occur as a result of recruitment techniques that fail to reach certain segments of the population, or are reaching them through different media. Muñoz reports that, in his experience, newspapers represent a more effective means of recruiting English than Spanish samples, while radio, television, and word-of-mouth have been more effective in attracting the latter. Media recruitment efforts in general appear to be ineffective in reaching blacks. Similarly, certain minority groups tend to be more skeptical than other groups, and, as a result, they respond less to warnings of immediate danger and other emergency messages.

Previous research has shown that volunteers, including survey respondents, tend to be better educated, higher in social class status, more intelligent, higher in need for social approval, and more sociable than nonvolunteers (Rosenthal & Rosnow, 1975). To the extent that these and other individual differences are related to the population variables being studied, estimates of parameters could be biased. As such, the generalizability of data obtained from using voluntary subjects exclusively would be threatened. In prevention research, for example, if samples of volunteer subjects tend to include individuals who are above average in intelligence, they might be better able to learn techniques for preventing interpersonal difficulties, depression, and so on than people with similar symptoms who do not volunteer. This could have the result of leading the researcher to overestimate the effectiveness of a prevention program. Of course, this may not be a significant problem if the program ultimately implemented on a widespread basis is voluntary.

## The Selection Problem

Randomization appears to be the fairest way of deciding who can participate in certain research projects, and to what extent they will be exposed to the social intervention, when the number of research participants is necessarily limited by budgetary and other concerns (Wortman & Rabinovitz, 1979). Investigators and research volunteers both seem to view random selection decided by lotteries as one of the fairest approaches for allowing access to programs for which there are more applicants than places available, and this approach seems to represent a reasonable compromise between ethical and methodological research requirements (Conner, 1982).

An unfortunate drawback of attempts to apply rigorous experimental methods, such as random selection or random assignment of subjects to groups in essentially unaltered areas of social reality, is that the investigator might be caught in a paradoxical situation. Criticism of randomized experiments in social research on grounds pertaining to the ethics of experimentation is such that the scientist is placed in a "Catch-22" position. While some critics argue that untreated control group subjects are unfairly denied the benefits of a potentially effective program, others argue that treated, experimental group subjects are unfairly subjected to questionable, potentially harmful treatments. The dilemma is that experimentation in social research may be viewed as unfair, whether the treatment is found to be helpful or harmful (Kidder & Judd, 1986). Similarly, Muñoz (1983) has warned that an intervention found to have significant impact on almost all of the people it reaches would run the risk of appearing manipulative or coercive, in that the cause of the changes would likely be attributed to the power of the method rather than the volition of those who are changed. A method found to have an effect on a smaller percentage of subjects might be viewed as more appropriate from the perspective of subjects' individual freedom, whereas ineffective techniques would simply be viewed as failures.

## Untreated Control Groups

When experimental treatment designs are applied to social research investigations, ethical decisions must be made regarding the use of untreated control groups and comparison groups in which the effects of a new intervention are either unknown or potentially harmful. To a great extent, those decisions ultimately depend upon the relative value of the treatment and current alternatives, both as determined from prior research and predicted before the study is conducted, and the immediate need of participants for treatment.

Assigning subjects to an untreated control group raises an ethical problem basically similar to that encountered with placebo groups and untreated control patients in pharmacological research. Social intervention researchers tend to agree that the random assignment of persons to an untreated control group is defensible, even in cases where subjects fail to receive a benefit that would have been gained had they been assigned to an experimental group, as long as the benefit was discovered only *after* the results were analyzed (Campbell & Cecil, 1982; Schuler, 1982). However, when some direct loss to untreated controls can be foreseen prior to the study, their inclusion may be partly indefensible. This issue is potentially complicated in cases where failing to receive a benefit is experienced as a loss by those affected. One might also expect a methodological problem to arise as a consequence of the random assignment if untreated controls become disappointed about their relative deprivation. Should this occur, more subjects in the control group may be lost during the experiment, thereby causing a differential attrition rate.

It is recommended here that the social intervention investigator not be unduly concerned with the apparent ethical undesirability of depriving the control group of a potentially beneficial intervention. Such deprivation typically is but a "focal deprivation," made salient by the existence of the experimental group. Except perceptually, control group participants would *not* be less deprived were the experiment to be canceled and no one get the beneficial intervention. Many such experiments will be worthless for determining the efficacy of the intervention unless there is a "deprived" control group, and so should be canceled if none is permitted. Overall, the ethical value of information on possible interventions outweighs the *perceived* deprivation (so perceived by themselves or others) of untreated controls, though this must be decided on a case-by-case basis.

The use of untreated controls can be further justified in that there no doubt will be many research situations in which the intervention cannot reasonably be offered to everyone in need because of a lack of resources (e.g., Gueron, 1985). Diener and Crandall (1978) have used this point to justify the inclusion of untreated, randomly assigned control subjects in Head Start programs for deprived preschoolers. In their view, although placed at a disadvantage, the control group subjects were like thousands of other disadvantaged children around the nation whom the investigators could not possibly have been expected to help. Of course, untreated controls often differ from untreated individuals outside the experiment, in that the former are sometimes uninformed that they are control subjects and have been led to expect help.

Other cases where untreated control groups would be acceptable in studies of known positive interventions are those in which subjects can experience the successful intervention once the research is completed, as long as they do not suffer substantially in the meantime as a result of the withholding of a required treatment (see Boruch & Wothke, 1985). Many researchers, particularly those in the helping professions, no doubt will feel an obligation to aid untreated controls who have assisted them in their research upon completion of a study.

## Labeling: A Negative Effect of
## Early Subject Identification

In Chapter 2, the problem of labeling in preventive intervention research was briefly described. Again, a labeling effect essentially is a negative self-fulfilling prophecy that comes about as a result of early identification of persons at risk. The probability of labeling effects can be reduced by appropriate alternative research strategies. For example, in order to avoid labeling effects in classrooms where specific children are identified as research subjects who are "at risk," Jason and Bogat (1983) recommend that an entire classroom of youngsters experience an intervention, with none identified as the specific target of the project. At the conclusion of the intervention the researchers could ascertain whether those youngsters who initially were lagging in basic skills had progressed in performance. Thus the success of the intervention would be determined without resulting in potentially damaging labeling effects. A difficult issue related to this suggestion, however, is the extent to which parents are asked to give permission for their children to participate in a classroomwide intervention. Degree of parental consent might vary depending on whether the intent of the project is described as educational (designed to increase useful learning skills) or psychological (designed to prevent clinical disorders) in nature (Muñoz, 1983).

## Other Solutions to
## the Labeling Problem

The likelihood of labeling effects no doubt is greatly reduced in research designs that address treatments to whole school rooms of children, as Jason and Bogat suggest, or groups that are designated publicly anyway, as with intervention efforts designed to prevent psychological problems among unemployed samples. As an illustration of such an approach, regional "broadcast" designs encompass those mental health preventive interventions where the treatment is to be delivered to regions, or institutions, rather than to specific persons at risk. With these interventions, the mental health services and outreach in a public school may be greatly augmented with an early diagnosis and treatment approach to prevention. Radio and television programs designed for preventive intervention research have been attempted, including the ongoing research by Jerome Johnston and associates utilizing educational television within classrooms (Granville, Johnston, & Nolan, 1983; Johnston, Blumenfeld, & Isler, 1983; Watkins, Perloff, Wortman, & Johnston, 1983). Unfortunately, in order to ascertain the impact of intervention on the average member of the target population adequately, comparable subsamples in an untreated comparison population typically must be located and incorporated into the research design, thereby limiting its practicality in reducing probable labeling effects. For example, in the hypothetical case of an early intensive intervention preventive mental health staffing of a pilot school, labeling effects would be a likely cost in a control school where untreated at-risk children are identified by teachers, and the children's names are kept available for follow-up.

One type of recommended alternative design that might preclude the need to designate untreated eligibles in a comparison group and, in fact, may enable researchers to do away with a comparison group entirely, thereby greatly limiting the likelihood of labeling, is the *regression-discontinuity design* (Campbell & Kimmel, 1985). Use of this design, consistent with other preventive intervention research designs, requires rigid assignment to treatments, but with the advantage that those getting the treatment are those scored as most needy. Classroom teachers, for example, could be asked to nominate children most needing early preventive intervention. The report form would include multiple ratings and poolings of ratings across survey periods, and across multiple teachers of the same child (if appropriate). An overall eligibility score thus would be generated. Up to staff and facility capacity, treatment would be given to the neediest as judged by this score, and those beyond the cutoff would receive no intervention. For *all* cases, treated and untreated, the eligibility score would be recorded, and employed as a crucial variable in analyzing posttest and other follow-up measures. From within the group receiving treatment, the slope of outcome scores on eligibility scores would be computed. Its intercept at the cut-off point would then be used as an estimate for what the treated-group mean would have been had there been a tie-breaking randomized assignment experiment for those in a class-interval around the cutting point. From those beyond the cutting point, the intercept of the slope of outcome on eligibility score would represent the untreated group of such a tie-breaking randomization. It is those untreated closest to the cutting point that are most crucial, and there is little point in following up on those most remote from that point. Perhaps a rule of using twice the eligibility-unit span of the treated group could be employed. Absolute numbers are important, to give stability to the slope estimates. Introductions to this design are provided in Campbell (1969) and Cook and Campbell (1979), while Trochim (1982) has provided a book-length treatment.

While recommended as an approach likely to limit the occurrence of labeling, the regression-discontinuity design is not without other potential ethical problems. It does require administrative recognition that it likely will not be possible to treat intensively and effectively all those who might benefit from the intervention. The decision has to be made to treat those treated at full strength, up to staff capacity, and to give others no treatment at all. This treatment shortage could be used to divide randomly a larger needy group into treated and untreated groups. However, while scientifically ideal, this can produce perceived unfairness, in that equally needy cases are going untreated.

It should be noted that there are some critics of labeling theory who believe that the power of labels is overstated (e.g., Gove, 1980, 1982). However, it is assumed here that labeling effects represent a serious ethical concern for social intervention researchers. It is suggested that all interventions running the risk of labeling effects be avoided. Also, it would be beneficial for social researchers to begin to develop short-term measures of labeling as precursors of labeling effects. For example, early indicators of labeling might be obtained by asking teachers and parents to identify children most needing early preventive intervention. Similar early indicators could be obtained about employees in organizations from coworkers, about recently separated adults from neighbors, and so on.

## SUMMARY

In conclusion, coping with the labeling effect and other issues pertaining to the selection and assignment of research participants is viewed as a compromise between the social imperative of human rights and the methodological requirements of applied research. Such compromises are made in the spirit of scientific advancement in that they challenge researchers to seek alternative methodological strategies and research designs that protect their subjects' rights. There is always the possibility, however, that ethical standards and IRB review will be viewed as hurdles that are impossible to clear, and will have a "chilling" effect on researchers, inhibiting them from asking important questions and from conducting certain kinds of research that pose methodological/ethical dilemmas (e.g., studies on obedience). Inhibiting research in order to avoid such dilemmas is contrary to the goals of applied social research and scientific progress.

## RECOMMENDED READINGS

Cook, T. D., & Campbell, D. T. (1979). *Quasi-experimentation: Design and analysis issues for field settings.* Boston: Houghton Mifflin.
Faden, R. R., & Beauchamp, T. L. (1986). *A history and theory of informed consent.* New York: Oxford University Press.
Price, R. H., Ketterer, R. F., Bader, B. C., & Monahan, J. (Eds.). (1982). *Prevention in mental health: Research, policy, and practice.* Beverly Hills, CA: Sage.
Rosenthal, R., & Rosnow, R. L. (Eds.). (1969). *Artifact in behavioral research.* New York: Academic Press.
Schuler, H. (1982). *Ethical problems in psychological research.* New York: Academic Press.

## CHAPTER EXERCISES

1. *Case Study:* A psychologist has been hired by an organization to implement a recently developed intervention program for the treatment of alcohol and drug abusers. Employees who are suspected by management to be experiencing drug- or alcohol-related problems that are affecting their performance at work will be referred to the company's Employee Assistance Program—a program specifically designed for employee counseling—in order to receive the new treatment. Employees also will be allowed to enter the program voluntarily at any time. However, the Medical and Labor Relations departments of the organization are wary that employees who enter the program (either voluntarily or through referrals) will be labeled as "alcoholics" or "drug abusers" by management, which may result in unfair and unwarranted dismissal from their jobs. In addition, the psychologist is somewhat uncertain that the intervention program will have intended positive effects on employees treated, since the research evidence on its effectiveness has been mixed.

What ethical problems are posed by this case?

What sort of referral program would you recommend in order to protect against the labeling and unfair firings of employee-users of the treatment program?

To what extent should employees be informed about the intervention program?

# 5

# Confidentiality and
# the Right to Privacy

Privacy and confidentiality are two ethical issues that are crucial to social researchers who, by the very nature of their research, frequently request individuals to share with them their thoughts, attitudes, and experiences. When the questions pertain to sensitive topics, material risks to respondents may be attached to the providing of information, in addition to a depreciation of privacy (Boruch & Cecil, 1979). In a recent survey, social scientists in the evaluation profession rated protection of the confidentiality of individuals as one of the most important ethical issues in their field (Sheinfeld & Lord, 1981).

This chapter describes the major issues related to the recognition of respondents' right to privacy in social research and the assurance that the information they provide remains confidential. Following a definition of terms, the need for protecting individual privacy and confidentiality of data in social research is considered. Since privacy and confidentiality are most obviously pertinent—though not limited—to social survey research, their impact on consent and accuracy of response is reviewed. Strategies for protecting privacy and confidentiality—without seriously threatening the researcher's freedom to investigate social issues—are described, including statistical procedures for concealing the precise identity of research participants, and legal protections for those who provide sensitive information.

At least in part, the ethical social researcher is one who is aware of ways in which privacy and confidentiality may be jeopardized and safeguarded, and is knowledgeable about the effects of privacy and confidentiality on consent and the validity of survey findings. It is suggested that as privacy guidelines in society in general shift, so too will our evaluations of issues pertinent to the ethics of social research. Toward increasing awareness about these issues, it is first necessary to examine the more general concept of privacy (of which confidentiality is but one dimension) and the nature and goals of specific privacy situations.

## THE NATURE AND GOALS OF PRIVACY

*Privacy* has been defined by Alan Westin (1968, p. 7) as "the claim of individuals, groups, or institutions to determine for themselves when, how, and to what extent information about them is communicated to others." This definition regards privacy, when viewed in terms of the individual's relation to social participation, as voluntary and temporary withdrawal from others through physical or psychological means. Privacy and confidentiality differ in the sense that the former pertains to persons and the latter pertains to information and data. As an extension of privacy, *confidentiality* "refers to agreements between persons that limit others' access to private information" (Sieber, 1982a, p. 146). As such, a research participant might agree to reveal certain information to a social researcher, but only under circumstances in which the researcher agrees to limit access by others to data that can be linked to the participant.

Because of the assumed equally powerful need to participate in society, an individual's desire for privacy is never absolute, and one is continually engaged in a personal adjustment process in which the desire for privacy must be balanced against the desire for disclosure and personal communication with others. This adjustment occurs in the context of environmental conditions, including pressures from curious others (such as social scientists), as well as the society's norms and processes of surveillance used to enforce them.

Persons can maintain privacy by controlling who may enter into their lives and who may be privy to information about them (Sieber, 1982a). Thus if researchers reveal (wittingly or unwittingly) information about the attitudes, motivations, or behaviors that a research participant would rather not have revealed, the latter's basic right to privacy has been compromised and an ethical problem has been encountered. Moral theologians call such breaches of trust *detraction*, meaning any unjustified assertion about the good name of another, even though it is not formally untrue (Francis, 1982). The philosopher Thomas Aquinas, in his *Summa Theologica*, spoke of detraction as the depreciation of another's reputation by exposing secrets. Detraction differs, for example, from relationships in which an individual willingly agrees to forego his or her right to privacy. The protection of a person's honor and good name by not revealing what may be discreditable or embarrassing, and the elimination of undue inquisitiveness or prying, thus are central to the privacy issue. Considerations of detraction are firmly rooted in the modern concept of privacy and the basic conflict between the right to know and the right to privacy.

Westin (1968) has distinguished among four basic states of individual privacy, which differ in terms of whether a person's voluntary withdrawal is accomplished in a state of solitude or small-group intimacy or, when among larger groups, in a condition of anonymity or reserve. *Solitude* is the most complete state of privacy that can be achieved by an individual, in that a person is separated from the group and freed from the observation of others. This state of privacy might be sought for private thought, simple relaxation, or to engage in activities such as reading or writing. Solitude, however, is not to be confused with isolation, since an isolated person might seek unsuccessfully the company of others. As the intensities of everyday life continue to increase, some retreat into solitude is likely to become even more essential than it already is in our society. An illustration of solitude taken from the medical context can be found in the rest and quiet needed for complete recovery from an illness.

The second state of privacy, *intimacy*, obtains among small numbers of individuals, usually pairs, who attempt to achieve satisfactory personal relationships. Typical units of intimacy from which others are excluded include the obvious, such as lovers, families, and friendship circles, as well as work cliques, such as those in which collaborators conduct a joint project or individuals engage in delicate business negotiations. As defined by Westin, intimacy in the research setting is sometimes required in the investigator/participant relationship so that trust can grow and the participant can voluntarily reveal facts and emotions otherwise not disclosed. This state of privacy provides a circumstance for emotional release without the feeling of being culpable for one's remarks.

A third state of privacy is *anonymity*, which occurs when the individual seeks freedom from identification and surveillance in public settings. While related to solitude, anonymity is the desire of individuals for moments of "public privacy." In this state, a person chooses not to reveal who he or she is, and does not expect to be personally identified or held to the rules of role or behavior that would operate under normal conditions. In anonymous relations, one often can freely communicate with a stranger, safe in the understanding that the stranger cannot exert authority or restraint, and that subsequent interactions with the stranger are unlikely. Thus some confidences that are carefully withheld from a more closely related person might be readily revealed under conditions of anonymity.

In social and medical research, anonymity is most closely related to confidentiality, since anonymity would be lost if data were used in a way that led to the identification of a subject. A breach of privacy in this regard increases the possibility that subjects may be harmed. Individuals who view their psychological, physical, or economic condition as demeaning (such as victims of AIDS or welfare recipients) may choose to remain anonymous when visiting researchers' laboratories, clinics, or consulting rooms, although anonymity in such contexts often is not possible (e.g., they may have to identify themselves for Blue Cross or Medicaid in social or clinical intervention studies). The "Springdale" incident, discussed in Chapter 1, is an example of how failure to protect the anonymity of research participants may be potentially damaging to the individuals involved.

The fourth state of privacy, *reserve*, is the most subtle state, in that it represents the creation of a psychological barrier against unwanted intrusion. Reserve occurs when the individual's need to limit communications that reveal aspects of his or her innermost self is protected by the willing discretion of surrounding others. By maintaining a state of reserve while in a group, an individual might obtain needed moments of privacy through limited disclosure. Reserve often must be exercised in the medical setting by a doctor in order to protect the secrets of patients.

There are major international codes of human rights (such as the United Nations' Universal Declaration of Human Rights, and the European Convention on Human Rights) that specify the right to privacy, which also is implicit in all of the various American and European ethical codes for research and professional standards. Some common threads running throughout these codes are a fundamental respect for the person, redress from detraction, the need for anonymity, the protection of solitude and intimacy, and the prohibition of breaches of reserve and confidentiality. The principle that researchers should keep their subjects' data confidential is, in fact, one of only three principles that appear without exception in all American and European codes for psychological research and professional standards (the other two are to avoid physical harm and to avoid psychological harm) (Schuler, 1982). Nevertheless, attempts to apply these formal standards in certain contexts often give rise to difficult moral choices. Problems of application are especially evident in research and clinical practice where the need for information conflicts with the reluctance to disclose that information. To illustrate, psychology's current standards narrow the focus of privacy onto confidentiality:

Information obtained about the research participant during the course of an investigation is confidential unless otherwise agreed upon in advance. When the possibility exists that others may obtain access to such information, this possibility, together with plans for protecting confidentiality, is explained to the participant as part of the procedure for obtaining informed consent. (American Psychological Association, 1982, p. 7)

This principle reflects the position that one of the investigator's primary responsibilities is to fulfill subjects' expectations of anonymity and confidentiality, and that this obligation is intricately related to informed consent. But while it is intended to protect the anonymity of research subjects and require reserve on the part of the researcher, the principle fails to extend to the intimacy at the core of the researcher/subject relationship.

As discussed earlier, psychologists engaged in human subject research are sometimes confronted with a dilemma whereby informing their subjects about certain aspects of a study poses a threat to the validity of subjects' responses. While many researchers "resolve" this conflict either through the omission of pertinent information about one or more aspects of the research, or by misinforming subjects (i.e., conveying wrong information) through the use of deception, research subjects in turn may be reluctant to confess that they were *not* naive about the study. Disclosure of information on both sides could compromise or invalidate the subject's participation in the research and, as a result, a "pact of ignorance" may develop between the researcher and the subject, contrary to the best interests of intimacy in the relationship (Orne, 1962). When research subjects convey the nature of experimental deceptions or research hypotheses to friends or relatives who will later participate in the same study, the implicit cooperative agreement between researcher and subject will have been further breached. Prior information about the study can then be used by its recipient to improve his or her status in a relationship with the researcher. In this case, to be privy to privileged information potentially destroys the intimacy or trust that defines the role relationship in a scientific setting.

The legitimacy of revealing information about others despite promises to the contrary often depends upon the context in which the breach of confidence occurs (Kimmel, 1985b). The gossip of researchers at staff meetings and cocktail parties about the intimate relations of their subjects is morally reprehensible when such talk clearly will not serve to benefit the subject. But the breach of confidence that would be necessary to save the life of someone who confides plans of suicide no doubt would be viewed by most individuals as legitimate. A doctor who discusses a patient's illness with a social worker, because it appears that the patient needs social support as well as needed treatment, also would likely be viewed as ethically justifiable, particularly if the doctor and the social worker share a similar ethic in their loyalty to the patient, and have as their mutual aim the recovery or support of the patient.

Breaches of confidence that are constrained by known and acknowledged commitments of the professional people involved with a research participant, patient, or client have been labeled *convergent* by British physician H. W. S. Francis (1982). In contrast, breaches of confidence are *divergent* when they are not contained within a known group of continuing professional commitments. The circumstance in which a doctor introduces his or her patient to a research physician whose loyalty is not to the patient, but to the success of a research project, or to the greater good of humanity, is divergent because the doctor who passes on information also loses control of it. In this case, a fiduciary bond between the doctor and the patient that no adverse consequences will follow cannot be developed (a *fiduciary* relationship is one in which power is entrusted to one person for the benefit of another). Similarly, the social researcher who furnishes identified records to another analyst or auditor for reappraisal might later find that those records were passed on to another researcher and utilized in a study, albeit with the worthiest of intentions. Of course, even in the example of the social worker, the doctor cannot be absolutely certain that information will not be divulged within the social worker's professional circles. Even where risks to research participants are absent, the principles of privacy and confidentiality still obtain, although the acceptability of researchers' specific applications of these principles may depend on the context in which ethical choices are made.

## THE NEED TO PROTECT INDIVIDUAL
## PRIVACY AND CONFIDENTIALITY OF DATA

In measuring the success of social research efforts it is often necessary to collect data concerning subjects' economic and social status, home and family relationships, and mental and physical well-being over extended periods of observation (sometimes lasting for several months or years). The importance of experimentally evaluating social intervention effectiveness in long-term follow-ups is so great as to justify collecting and keeping available for use in follow-ups participants' names, addresses, social security numbers, parents' names, and so on, even though having these linkable to damaging information (e.g., about mental health or economic status) increases the risk of injurious leaks from members of the data-collection, record-keeping, and analysis staffs.

Confidentiality of an individual's responses can be threatened by disclosure by various means, such as government appropriation of a researcher's records, inadvertent disclosure of a record, casual interrogation, or theft (Boruch & Cecil, 1979). Thus ethical problems relevant to invasion of subjects' privacy and the extent to which confidentiality can be guaranteed for future use of the data become particularly salient.

## Ethical Conflicts Pertaining to Privacy and Confidentiality

While the occurrence of privacy questions and concerns in social research are hardly new, their incidence and character have changed, apparently as a result of changes in the focus, methods, and goals of social research. As Boruch and Cecil (1979) have observed, early public concern about privacy tended to center on census surveys and the government's use of resulting data. Eckler (1972), in his survey of the early history of social research in the United States, found the idea of protecting the confidentiality of data obtained for statistical purposes explicit in the 1840 U.S. Census Bureau guidelines, which required that census enumerators regard the information they obtained from respondents as confidential. In fact, throughout the existence of the U.S. Census Bureau, attempts have been made to assure that respondents' fear of disclosure would not inhibit cooperation in research. As the quality of social surveys improved over time, the laws governing disclosure of information have become much more explicit in requiring confidentiality in order to preserve the quality of data collected. According to Eckler, the same pattern can be seen in the early development of economic welfare statistics.

The nature of privacy concerns has changed over time as social scientists have become more involved in identifying social problems and testing possible solutions through field research (Boruch & Cecil, 1979). With an increase in the policy relevance of social research, a higher standard for empirical data has emerged, placing less emphasis on anecdote and expert opinion than in the past. These developments have generated conflicts about privacy with policymakers, research sponsors, groups of research participants, journalists, and others who are unfamiliar with the objectives and standards of the more sophisticated methods, and who tend to share opposing views on the value and implications of research.

Applications of social policy research have resulted in a number of recent conflicts about privacy issues. One incident that gave rise to considerable public and governmental concern occurred during the New Jersey negative income tax experiment, a social experiment designed to measure the impact of various negative income tax plans on families whose income was close to the poverty level (Baratz, 1973; Kershaw, 1975; Riecken & Boruch, 1974). Low-income families were supported by the state with sums (between $1,000 and $2,000 per year) representing various percentages of the poverty-level income. Participants were asked to complete detailed questionnaires about their income, work-related behavior, and other activities before, during, and after the experiment. The overall project has since been cited as an impressive study of economic, psychological, and sociological hypotheses, and a case exercise in the pitfalls social scientists can anticipate in applied policy research (Baratz, 1973). However, although participants were promised confidentiality, local law enforcement officers viewed the project as an opportunity to check on welfare cheating, and attempted to obtain the confidential information in order to expose tax and subsidy fraud. Records on identified subjects eventually were demanded by a grand jury and a congressional investigating committee. The researchers, having promised in good faith to protect respondents' data, were placed in a difficult position, uncertain as to whether that promise could be kept if a court issued a subpoena. The officials eventually were convinced through careful negotiations to discontinue their demands for relevant data.

Distressed by the dilemmas posed by the New Jersey income maintenance project, the U.S. Office of Economic Opportunity recommended that the Committee on Federal Agency Evaluation Research study the problem of confidentiality and recommended ways of ensuring the protection of data in future evaluations and social experiments. In their final report, the Committee presented the following recommendations:

(1) that all federal agencies engaging in evaluation research adopt rigorous procedures to ensure that data collected about individuals in the course of such research are kept strictly confidential and are not used for

purposes other than such research or released in any way that permits identification of individuals;
(2) that consideration be given to enactment of a federal statute that would protect from subpoena information collected from individuals in the course of federal evaluation research and thus prevent such information from being used in law enforcement or other legal proceedings. (Committee on Federal Agency Evaluation Research, 1975, p. 7)

As the negative income tax project illustrates, the ethical dilemma in economic research tends to be one that involves a conflict between the researcher's promise of confidentiality and the integrity of the research on one hand, and the interests of governmental investigators to administer justice (e.g., by auditing social research records) on the other (Boruch & Cecil, 1979). Similar conflicts between research and legal standards are prevalent in social research on other sensitive topics, such as drug use and criminal behavior. Boruch and Cecil (1979) have argued that the legitimate use of archival information by researchers may be impeded by the tendency of certain agencies (such as the Federal Bureau of Investigation) to refuse even the anonymous disclosure of information. While intended to protect confidentiality of data, such policies present barriers to rigorous social research requiring long-term follow-ups. In the area of juvenile delinquency research, legal threats of appropriation of records on identified research participants have been persistent (Brymer & Farris, 1967). Privacy-related conflicts such as these also are abundant in educational research. For example, new regulations designed to protect the privacy of students by restricting access to their school records (such as the Privacy Act of 1974 and the Family Educational Rights and Privacy Act of 1974) can, at the same time, prevent valuable educational research (e.g., studies to assess the impact of special educational programs and the effectiveness of teachers, curricula, and the like).

These and other ethical and legal conflicts highlight the importance of privacy and confidentiality in social research. In sum, Sieber (1982a) has identified six reasons why the protection of information obtained from research participants represents a major issue for social scientists:

(1) The possibility of disclosure of potentially embarrassing or secret information obtained from participants presents the risk of psychological, social, or economic harm to participants.
(2) Obtaining sensitive information for research purposes is legally protected only if participants' privacy rights are protected.
(3) The goals of research often require investigators to store data with unique identifiers (such as names and addresses) for long-term research.

(4) Research data can be subpoenaed by a court.
(5) The collection of sensitive information might be constrained by recently developed legal standards created to protect confidentiality.
(6) Research participants are often suspicious about the uses to which information they disclose to researchers will be put.

## The Impact of Confidentiality on Survey Research

Other arguments for the protection of privacy and confidentiality in social research are based more directly on scientific concerns than on ethical or legal grounds. The claim that data obtained from research participants ought to be kept confidential is commonly justified, in part, by the assumption that enhanced credibility or validity should result when the recipient promises to protect the confidentiality of disclosed information. By providing potential respondents with assurances of confidentiality, investigators also hope to increase the representativeness of their research findings by decreasing the likelihood of nonresponse in a subject sample. That is, the willingness of individuals to respond, if at all, to self-report social surveys, psychological tests, and attitude scales may depend very much on assurances provided by the researcher during the consent procedure. These considerations are particularly relevant for projects that involve sensitive or potentially embarrassing information—often the kind of information sought in social research. The empirical literature on these methodological issues is vast, and the intent here is to summarize briefly a few representative studies and their implications.

Studies on cooperation rates have tended to compare the response rates of research participants who have been assured confidentiality against the response data of an equivalent group of participants who have not. This is somewhat of an overly simplistic approach, in that cooperation rates can be expected to vary along with such factors as the nature of the assurance of confidentiality, strategies used to actualize the promise, and the sensitivity of the information requested from participants (Boruch & Cecil, 1979). However, in a review of the research related to the effects of variation in confidentiality and perceived anonymity on the responses received, Boruch (1975) found that certain patterns do tend to emerge. Respondents in studies who were presented with a promise of confidentiality that they understood and trusted were more likely to provide sensitive information (e.g., about drug use or abortions) than respondents who did not understand or trust the procedure utilized to secure confidentiality. According to Boruch, assurances of confidentiality seem to affect cooperation rates only when the information requested is sensitive in nature—similar assurances had no effect on the likelihood that subjects would provide innocuous information.

An aspect of Singer's (1978) investigation on the impact of informed consent on survey research (see Chapter 4) considered the effects of confidentiality on social survey response rates and response quality. Consistent with Boruch's (1975) conclusions, Singer found that an absolute assurance of confidentiality had a significant effect on nonresponse to specific questionnaire items. Respondents given an assurance of confidentiality had a lower nonresponse rate than subjects not provided with such assurances, despite the sensitive nature of the face-to-face interview.

Other studies specifically designed to evaluate alternative methods of assuring confidentiality suggest that a simple promise to participants that their responses will remain confidential may not be sufficient assurance to satisfy their needs for privacy. Reaser, Hartsock, and Hoehn (1975) and Zdep and Rhodes (1977) found that respondents were significantly more likely to admit undesirable behavior when the mechanism for preserving confidentiality was clear and respondents were provided with concrete, visible assurance that the promise would be maintained.

In order to provide better understanding of how cooperation rates vary in social research, a large-scale field experiment was carried out by the Panel on Privacy and Confidentiality as Factors in Survey Response, a multidisciplinary group established by the National Academy of Sciences (NAS). Beginning in 1976, the Panel investigated a national probability sample of respondents to determine the effects of privacy and confidentiality on their feelings about and response to household censuses and surveys. Participants in the project were randomly assigned to different assurance levels, ranging from permanent confidentiality of records to an explicit statement that replies may be given to other agencies. A rather weak relationship was revealed suggesting that as the level of confidentiality decreases, refusal rates tend to increase (Committee on National Statistics, 1979). Boruch and Cecil (1979) have conjectured that the weakness of the trend can be explained by the innocuous nature of the census surveys and by the likelihood that many respondents, especially in census interviews, simply expect to be assured of confidentiality. Postinterview responses in the NAS study provide indirect evidence for the latter explanation. Overall, a large majority of the 4,420 NAS respondents (76%) who were given assurance of confidentiality accurately recalled the characteristics of the assurance, while a substantial proportion of respondents (40%) not promised confidentiality erroneously recalled or assumed that their replies would be kept confidential. This suggests that individuals may carry an image of census surveys that lead them to presume that their responses will be protected, and that this presumption overrides what one is told by an interviewer during the consent stage of the research process.

In addition to research on cooperation rates, a number of studies also have been conducted to determine whether the promise of confidentially has an effect on the validity of data obtained from research participants. One approach has been for investigators to examine the extent to which respondents are likely to provide socially desirable responses to personality inventories under varying conditions of confidentiality. In a recent investigation, Esposito, Agard, and Rosnow (1984) studied the effects of conditions of confidentiality, anonymity, and nonanonymity on subjects' tendency to give socially desirable responses to a self-report personality measure (the State-Trait Anxiety Inventory). Respondents in the *confidentiality* condition were asked to give their names, but were promised that their responses would be kept strictly confidential. Those in the *anonymity* condition were not asked for their names and there was no statement regarding confidentiality. In the *nonanonymity* condition respondents' names were requested and again there was no statement about confidentiality. The findings revealed that a written assurance to subjects that their responses would be kept strictly confidential substantially reduced the likelihood of response distortion due to socially desirable responding. Anonymity without the promise of confidentiality, however, had no appreciable effect when compared with nonanonymity alone.

Other researchers have reported that more candid responses are obtained about potentially embarrassing topics, such as birth control practices and child abuse, when respondents are certain that the promise of confidentiality can be sustained, but not when the devices for assuring confidentiality appear to be weak (e.g., Krotki & Fox, 1974; Liu, Chow, & Mosley, 1975; Zdep & Rhodes, 1977). The more effective strategies for actualizing confidentiality were those that utilized a statistical method (such as the randomized response method, described below) in contrast to more conventional interview methods. But there also is evidence that the use of concrete assurances of confidentiality will not always improve the validity of subjects' responses to sensitive areas. Negligible differences between rates of admitting drug use under varying conditions of confidentiality have been reported in studies of Army officers (Brown & Harding, 1973) and college students (King, 1970). Similarly, Folsom (1974) found that a simple promise of confidentiality was slightly more acceptable than a more convincing approach that relied on a complex statistical method for assuring the promise in obtaining responses about drinking and driving. It is unclear why additional assurances of confidentiality did not have a more substantial effect on candor in these studies, although it has been suggested that the novelty of the approaches to assure confidentiality may have aroused suspicion in respondents rather than cooperation (Boruch & Cecil, 1979).

In sum, one general finding that emerges from the empirical literature is that some potential respondents in research on sensitive topics will refuse to cooperate when an assurance of confidentiality is weak, vague, not understood, or thought likely to be breached. Thus it appears that the usefulness of data in sensitive research areas may be seriously affected by the investigator's ability to provide a credible promise of confidentiality. Assurances do not appear to affect cooperation rates in innocuous studies, perhaps due to prior expectation on the part of most potential respondents that confidentiality will be protected. Promises of confidentiality of data apparently can pay off in terms of increased validity of some self-report measures in social research. But promises of confidentiality alone may not be sufficient to improve response without a consideration of other stimulus and situational variables.

## STRATEGIES FOR PROTECTING
## PRIVACY AND CONFIDENTIALITY

An individual's responses obtained during a social research investigation are regarded as confidential when identifiable information (i.e., information that includes a name, address, or other forms of unique identification) is not revealed by the researcher to others. A wide variety of procedures have been developed to help ensure that promises of confidentiality are protected, some of which are described below. The various strategies correspond to two distinct risks to the privacy of individuals who provide information about themselves to researchers (Committee on Federal Agency Evaluation Research, 1975). The risk of *unauthorized misuse* of sensitive data involves the possibility that identifiable information collected for research purpose might be obtained by unauthorized persons (such as blackmailers, sales people, and bill collectors) and used against an individual. Here the problem for the researcher is how to provide *physical protection* of the data, either by reducing the number of persons with access to identifiable records, or by devising strategies to destroy the link between identifiers and responses.

The other risk is that of *official misuse* of sensitive data for law enforcement or other official purposes. The problem here is how to provide *legal protection* for respondents so that they can be assured that the information they provide about their behavior cannot and will not be used for other purposes.

## Physical Protection

One of the most basic means for protecting the privacy of research participants is to avoid sensitive or embarrassing questions or else limit their number by including only those that are clearly necessary to the research and will be used. When feasible, anonymity of respondents should be preserved as early in the research process as possible by omitting or not collecting identifying information. Unfortunately, these procedures would limit the usefulness and validity of many studies because of the nature of social research questions and the need to check and follow up data.

A number of useful statistical techniques have been suggested for safeguarding data when the deletion of direct personal identifiers is insufficient to preserve confidentiality. Included among these are *microaggregation methods* (Feige & Watts, 1970), whereby data on many synthetic average persons are created and released as a substitute for individual data. Microaggregation methods are potentially useful for assuring confidentiality of archival data and for eliciting information directly from individuals in survey situations. For these methods, the released records contain averaged information of the individual subjects within each aggregate, thereby protecting the anonymity of individual records, while providing the researcher the opportunity to apply descriptive and inferential statistics to the data.

Other statistical strategies to preserve the confidentiality of individual responses in certain survey situations (such as face-to-face interviews and more impersonal settings) include *randomized response methods,* (Greenberg, Horvitz, & Abernathy, 1974; Tracy & Fox, 1981; Warner, 1965, 1971) and *error inoculation methods* (Boruch, 1972), in which data are "contaminated" in various ways with random errors. In a simple variant of the randomized response approach, interviewers record the answer to a randomly determined question so that they are unable to determine the question that any given respondent is actually answering. To illustrate, Tracy and Fox (1981) have suggested that in order to estimate the prevalence, for example, of wife abuse—a behavior that might be of primary interest to the social researcher and one that is likely to generate a legal risk or embarrassment to a disclosing respondent—the question, for example, "Did you beat your wife last month?" should be followed by an innocuous question in the same Yes-No format as the stigmatizing question, for example, "Did you use a public telephone last week?" Each respondent in a sample of married men could then be instructed to select one of the questions randomly and to answer it truthfully without revealing which question was chosen. In this way, a respondent is protected by the fact that it is impossible for the researcher (and other respondents) to determine whether he used a public telephone or abused his spouse. On a probability basis, it is possible to obtain an estimate—in this case, of the prevalence of wife abuse—without compromising the respondent's right to privacy.

Continuing with the above example, suppose that the researchers previously have determined the probability (e.g., 50%) of public telephone use by married men, and that of 100 married men asked to respond to the two questions 60 raise a hand. It can be assumed that 50 of the hand raisers used a public telephone during the past week (regardless of whether or not they had abused their wives), and that the other 10 had not used a public telephone but had abused their wives. Since it can be assumed that 50 respondents did not use a public telephone during the past week, 10 out of 50, or 20%, is the estimate of the prevalence of wife abuse. With this strategy, it is impossible to discern which of the married men who raised their hands are the 20 who abused their wives. This is an oversimplified illustration of the logic of the randomized response method, and the interested reader should be aware that more complex versions of the method had been developed that can be practically applied in field research (see Boruch & Cecil, 1982; Fox & Tracy, 1984). Recently, Fox and Tracy (1984) have demonstrated how the unrelated question model of randomized response described above can be reformulated into a measurement error model, which in turn allows for a variety of multivariate analyses. Randomized response techniques have been demonstrated in research on fertility control, drug abuse, racial attitudes, and other sensitive topics.

Similar to the randomized response strategies are error inoculation methods, which also are useful for obtaining responses to sensitive variables, such as drug use or abortion, while preserving a respondent's confidentiality. One form of error inoculation useful for dichotomous variables involves random score substitution, whereby a random number is drawn to determine if a respondent's data are to be left as is or substituted, and a second random number is then selected to determine the substitute response. Because the researcher controls the general character of the error, he or she can estimate important statistical parameters from a large sample of respondents (such as how many have used a drug, have had an abortion, and so on) without knowing which particular responses are true or false.

There is some concern that such contamination procedures may not yet be usable in actual research (Schuler, 1982). Respondents who do not understand statistics may not trust the procedure, whereas those individuals who are sophisticated about statistics would clearly understand that the researchers could also calculate the probability that they have a police record or something else to hide. Further, the procedure might provide a first clue to respondents of the intimate nature of the questions, thereby raising their threshold of responsiveness. These contamination methods do, however, appear to function quite well in the contamination of stored data (Schuler, 1982). For more complete descriptions of these and other confidentiality-preserving techniques, as well as consideration of their limitations, readers should consult the excellent reviews by Boruch and Cecil (1982) and Campbell, Boruch, Schwartz, and Steinberg (1977).

## Legal Protection

During the last several years, the likelihood that researchers will be legally compelled to reveal information collected from participants in social research has increased, thus posing a new threat to the confidentiality of data. The New Jersey negative income experiment mentioned above and other incidents demonstrate that researchers can no longer promise in good faith that data will not be used for official purposes, including law enforcement, unless they have a legal basis for the promise (Committee on Federal Agency Evaluation Research, 1975). Although information can be subpoenaed by a court, researchers can protect themselves from potential dilemmas by petitioning federal or state agencies for protection from subpoena (Fowler, 1984).

The role of the government in privacy-related problems prior to 1970 largely was a reactive one. In January 1966, the President's Office of Science and Technology appointed the Panel on Privacy and Behavioral Research to examine the propriety of certain procedures in behavioral research and to propose guidelines for those engaged in such research. Restricting its attention to issues of privacy (defined as "the right of the individual to decide for himself how much he will share with others his thoughts, his feelings, and the facts of his personal life"), the Panel clearly stated the conflict between the individual's right to dignity, self-respect, and freedom, on the one hand, and society's right of discovery in view of restrictions that could curtail important research, on the other (Panel on Privacy and Behavioral Research, 1967, p. 536). The Panel notes that while most research does not violate the individual's right to privacy, there have been enough serious exceptions to warrant increased attention to procedures that protect this right.

By 1970, the Congress had enacted statutes that empowered the secretary of the Department of Health and Human Services (formerly, HEW), the U.S. Attorney General, and other governmental officials, to authorize persons engaged in research to protect the privacy of their research participants by withholding their identifying characteristics from others (Knerr, 1982). While these statutes do provide some protection for segments of the behavioral and social science research community, the protection afforded in each case is rather limited and somewhat ill-defined. Recently, however, the government's role has been enlarged as a result of legislative and bureaucratic interest in privacy. This interest seems to have come about as a result of some laws, such as the Privacy Act of 1974, and earlier attempts by various agency officials to establish ethical research policies (Boruch & Cecil, 1979).

The Privacy Act of 1974 complicates access to data on individuals maintained by the federal government and its contractors that had been facilitated by the Freedom of Information Acts of the late 1960s. The 1974 law, enacted in part to protect against violations of individual rights caused by incompetent record keeping, provides a set of rules for the collection, maintenance, and dissemination of information. Like the Family Educational Rights and Privacy Act, which was designed to protect information about students, the Privacy Act has aroused concern in social research spheres that it presents unnecessary constraints on the research process by curtailing the collection of useful information.

In short, the Privacy Act limits the extent to which researchers are able to obtain identifiable records from federal agencies. Other more recent federal and state statutes have been enacted to help assure that researchers who collect sensitive information from their participants will not be legally required to disclose it. These statutes protect data collected for research into alcohol and drug abuse, criminal behavior, and mental health areas. Examples include the statute prohibiting disclosure of Census records (13 U.S.C. 8, 9), and the limited protection provided for all individually identifiable information collected by the National Center for Health Statistics (42 U.S.C. 242m). Limited protection also is provided for patient records maintained in connection with drug abuse programs or research activities conducted, regulated, or assisted by a federal agency or department (42 U.S.C. 4582; 21 U.S.C. 1175). But while some research organizations routinely promise confidentiality of information collected, such guarantees tend not to have legal standing because the relation between researcher and respondent ordinarily is not recognized as privileged. Since space does not permit further discussion here of the complex legal issues pertinent to confidentiality, it is suggested that readers consult the comprehensive reviews provided by Boruch and Cecil (1979, chap. 8), Knerr (1982), and Nejelski (1976), which describe the various state and federal statutes protecting the confidentiality of certain types of data and advise how social researchers can secure protection of their data from subpoena.

## SUMMARY

Difficult choices arise in social research when the implications of what has been disclosed conflict with the reluctance to divulge sensitive information. Because of the desirability of long-term follow-up in order to obtain ideal outcome measures for many applied studies, there is little reason to expect that problems relating to confidentiality and the right to privacy will diminish in the future. Thus it is a major responsibility of the applied social researcher to prepare the basis for the protection of their subjects' privacy rights in anticipation of later follow ups. In this regard, it is recommended that (1) identifying information obtained from subjects (e.g., names, addresses, place of birth, social security numbers) should be recorded and archived under confidentiality-preserving conditions, and (2) the possibility of long-term follow-up should be mentioned routinely as part of the informed consent procedure (Campbell & Kimmel, 1985). Further, as decisions increasingly are made outside the social research professions in the legislative arena, it also is in the best interests of social researchers to continue to pursue methods for balancing public interests in social information with the parallel concerns for protecting individual privacy.

## RECOMMENDED READINGS

Barnes, J. A. (1979). *Who should know what? Social science, privacy and ethics.* Cambridge, England: Cambridge University Press.

Boruch, R. F., & Cecil, J. S. (1979). *Assuring the confidentiality of social research data.* Philadelphia: University of Pennsylvania Press.

Committee on National Statistics. (1979). *Privacy and confidentiality as factors in survey response.* Washington, DC: National Academy of Sciences.

Sieber, J. E. (Ed.). (1982). *The ethics of social research: Surveys and experiments (Part II). Survey research and protection of privacy and confidentiality.* New York: Springer-Verlag.

## CHAPTER EXERCISES

*Case Study:* A researcher who was a full-time employee of a company conducted an attitude survey in one of the company plants at the time of a union organizing drive. The announced purpose of the survey was to disclose any dissatisfaction with employment in the plant. The usual guarantee of anonymity was given to the participants. In the course of the study the researcher was able to identify certain individuals or groups with strong pro-union feelings. This information, if furnished to the plant manager, could have been of value in combating the organization drive.

(1) What is the moral dilemma or ethical problem in the study? Should the study have been conducted as described or should it have been developed differently?

(2) What steps should the researcher take to protect the confidentiality of information obtained from participants in the study?

# 6

# Special Problems
# in Applied Settings

This chapter focuses on some of the special problems inherent in the conduct of social research in applied settings. When social and behavioral scientists conduct their research in organizations and other real-life settings, evaluate ongoing social programs and prevention efforts, or assume an adversary role in their applied work, they often encounter unique and somewhat disconcerting ethical problems. Examples of these problems are presented below, along with a consideration of the responsibilities of social researchers in the control and application of their discoveries. A primary focus here is on the problems that arise when new scientific knowledge is misused or when widely accepted procedures and principles with proven utility are improperly implemented. The inappropriate utilization of research findings outside clearly stated limiting conditions can have serious and far-reaching consequences, and raises some important questions about the ethics of situations in which social researchers consult with and report their data to organizations, human service and community agencies, legal and educational officials, and the like.

## ETHICAL ISSUES IN
## ORGANIZATIONAL RESEARCH

Applied social scientists often are employed by organizations to conduct research in a number of areas. Many investigations in the organizational setting have as their goal the design and evaluation of programs to improve employee satisfaction and motivation, while others consist of the implementation of interventions designed to improve employee performance and relations. Another organizational research focus is directed toward personnel-related issues, including the validation of selection instruments and the testing and appraisal of employees for personnel decisions. In conducting these investigations, researchers and consultants from psychology and related fields may seek to improve an organization's capacities to achieve various goals (e.g., profit for a private business and delivery of services for a government agency), its employees' quality of work life, or the impact of the organization on other institutions or communities in the larger society (Walton, 1978).

When research professionals with advanced degrees enter into industrial/organizational settings for these and other purposes, they are expected to abide by the ethical standards and principles of conduct set forth by their professional organizations (e.g., the American Psychological Association) and/or federal and state statutes (as in the case of an individual licensed by a state to practice psychology). Although nonprofessionals who conduct organizational research, evaluation, and development are not formally responsible for adhering to professional standards, they often belong to professional associations (such as the American Society for Personnel Administrators) and typically are expected to follow many of the same standards that apply for professional scientists (London & Bray, 1980). Among the standards that are pertinent to researchers in organizations (in addition to those described in Chapter 3) are the American Psychological Association's generic *Standards for Providers of Psychological Services* (APA, 1977) and the supplementary *Speciality Guidelines for the Delivery of Services by Industrial/Organizational Psychologists* (APA, 1981b). These documents specify the researcher's obligation to protect the rights of the users of psychological services (including job applicants, employees, and the organization employing the researcher), to establish a system to protect the confidentiality of records, and to anticipate and resolve conflicts of interest arising from user relationships. More specialized technical guidelines are presented in the *Standards for Educational and Psychological Tests* (APA, 1974; currently being updated) and the *Principles for the Validation and Use of Personnel Selection Procedures* (Society for Industrial and Organizational Psychology, Inc., 1987).

While intended to provide ethical guidance for research and practice, adherence to these professional standards, coupled with the best of moral intentions, tends to be inadequate in preventing ethical dilemmas in organizational research. In one's attempt to conduct high-quality research, the pressures to comply with both professional and company standards (and the reality of organizational life), place considerable constraints on the organizational researcher (Angell, 1967; London & Bray, 1980). The realities of research in organizations are such that investigators are likely to become entangled in a set of multiple roles that give rise to ambiguous and conflicting expectations. For example, a social scientist might disapprove of the goals and strategies of an organization he or she is assisting, or question the fairness and justification of certain managerial actions (Walton, 1978). Similarly, a researcher might be asked to implement an intervention that has consequences that conflict with his or her values. These types of inconsistencies are likely to present ethical dilemmas for the researcher.

One such dilemma has been reported by an industrial psychologist who had been commissioned by management of a company to survey employee opinions and morale (Muchinsky, 1983). Although the respondents had been promised confidentiality, one survey response revealed the existence of employee theft. The psychologist thus was faced with the dilemma of having to tell management that some theft had occurred but that the employees involved could not be identified (when, in actuality, identification could have been made with relatively little effort), or alternatively to ignore it and fail to tell management about a serious company problem. Ethical dilemmas such as this tend not to have obvious solutions, in large part because of the complexity of the applied contexts in which they arise.

In their analysis of ethical relationships in organizations, Mirvis and Seashore (1982) argued that the very nature of an organization's social system necessitates that researchers approach their participants and attempt to resolve ethical dilemmas differently than they do in nonapplied contexts. This is because organizations (and other applied situations) consist not only of individuals who have hierarchical positions in relation to one another, but who collectively in their identity as an organization have relationships with supporters, consumers, government, unions, and other public institutions. In this context, research participants cannot be approached as independent individuals, nor can separate ethical guidelines be applied in dealing with employees, managers, sponsors, or clients, because all of these individuals behave within an interdependent framework of rights and responsibilities. It is likely that these individuals will have overlapping interests that sometimes are in conflict. Within this larger and more powerful context, investigators typically lack the power and means for singlehandedly managing ethical dilemmas or for invoking final authority to make decisions that affect the well-being of subjects and assurances that the research will be carried out as planned (see Weiss, 1978).

Mirvis and Seashore suggest that a consideration of roles and role relationships is useful for understanding and moderating ethical dilemmas in organizational research. In their view, the challenge of being ethical in organizations does not lie in the application of prescriptive guidelines and standards, but rather in the process of developing and maintaining research relationships in which to address ethical dilemmas. This approach requires a consideration of research participants in their roles as employees, managers, and members of an organization and society, and whose relationships in the organization are largely maintained by the role expectations they have for one another. Accordingly, a social scientist who enters an organizational context in the role of researcher has a responsibility to communicate his or her own role expectations to others, while at the same time accepting their expectations. In so doing, the interests of all parties can become clarified and the risks and potential benefits of alternative courses of action openly considered.

The nature of the role system that characterizes organizational research, as conceptualized by Mirvis and Seashore, is portrayed in Figure 6.1. The relationship between the researcher and participants in the organization is depicted as an intersection of their individual role systems. These role systems in turn fall within the larger system of American society with its corresponding ethical norms of freedom, equity, self-determination, due process, and so on. At the region of the researcher/participants intersection, new roles and role relations are created through the mutual communication of role expectations. Because researchers bring to this setting their own existing role relations with colleagues, their scientific profession, and users and sponsors of the research, they are likely to be confronted with a variety of disparate and seemingly incompatible expectations. For example, sponsors of an investigation might hold one set of expectations for the researcher, while the institution that employs the researcher holds another. Factions in the organization might have yet other expectations. It thus becomes the researcher's responsibility to clarify his or her own role in the situation—to study the organization unobtrusively, to test experimentally an intervention, to assist the organization in meeting various goals, or some combination of these. According to Mirvis and Seashore, by clarifying one's choice of role and openly communicating it to participants, a social scientist becomes better able to define his or her ethical responsibilities in an applied setting, to anticipate the risks and benefits of an investigation, and to distinguish the corresponding responsibilities of others. Similar clarifications for policy research have been recommended by social scientists (e.g., Fischer, 1980; Wildavsky, 1979).

To illustrate how these concepts can be applied to an actual research situation, Mirvis and Seashore described a field experiment conducted in a branch of a large metropolitan bank. An information system was

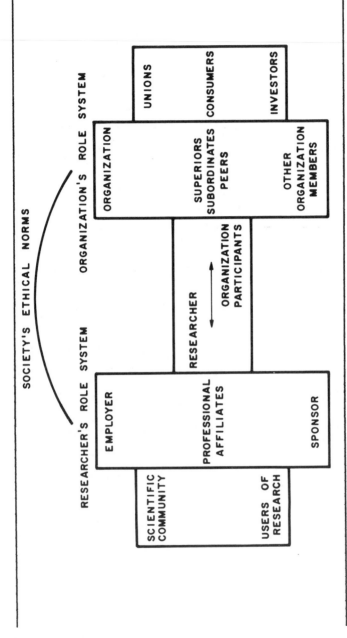

Figure 6.1  Organizational Research Role System

SOURCE: Mirvis, P. H., & Seashore, S. E. (1982). Creating ethical relationships in organizational research. In J. E. Sieber (Ed.), *The ethics of social research: Surveys and experiments* (p. 82). New York: Springer-Verlag. Reprinted by permission.

developed for gathering financial, behavioral, and attitudinal data (from records and directly from employees), to be returned periodically to work groups for problem solving and decision making. The researchers worked with a task force of bank employees to implement the program and later evaluated its effects on employees' performance and participation. However, a number of ethical questions arose during the study. Certain bank managers who felt that the program usurped some of their managerial powers resented the information system, while others who chose not to be involved in the project felt they had no choice in adopting the program. Although steps were taken to protect the confidentiality of data collected for the information system, there were concerns on the part of both participants and researchers that top management would ask to see the branch reports. In proposing the program and working closely with bank officials to implement it, the researchers chose an active role that was contrary to the detached and objective approach recommended by their scientific profession. Further questions were raised about how voluntary consent, privacy, and confidentiality were to be defined in this context and the means by which benefits were to be weighed against risks of providing treatments or interpretations of data that could negatively affect the status of some employees' jobs.

Most of the problems encountered by the researchers in this example can be traced to conflicting role expectations. From the researchers' role system came a set of expectations defining their professional responsibilities to obtain the voluntary informed consent of participants, protect the confidentiality of data, and involve employees and management participatively in the joint design of the project. But from the outset, managers and employees attempted to fit the researchers into preconceived role models already familiar to the firm. Upper management, for example, viewed them as inexpensive consultants whose job was to improve branch performance and morale. As such, they felt it appropriate to review confidential reports in order to stimulate further improvements. Many employees, by contrast, viewed the researchers as partisans who provided them with a direct channel of communication to management and, in one case, an opportunity to resist a branch manager's decision. This latter situation was seen by some managers as a threat to their effectiveness and control, and they reacted by using the data to remove uncooperative employees. Throughout the study, then, the researchers were faced with powerful pressures to conform to the competing role expectations of the various parties involved.

The difficulties that arose in the bank project, as in other studies, perhaps could have been avoided through an initial process of role definition, clarification, and resolution of conflict. In short, it is the investigator's responsibility as ethical decision maker "*to create roles that are mutually clarified and compatible and, in creating them, to affirm general ethical norms governing human research*" (Mirvis & Seashore, 1982, p. 91; their emphasis). This requires a recognition of the intersection of role systems and resolution of problems "through collaborative effort and appeal to common, transcendent goals" (p. 84). Should researchers and consultants determine that the values of a client organization are unacceptable and cannot be changed, it may be best to leave the situation entirely (Pfeiffer & Jones, 1977). In such cases, subsequent conflicts among role expectations might be unresolvable, and overly frustrating for all parties involved.

## ETHICS AND EVALUATION:
## SOME ILLUSTRATIVE PROBLEMS

*Evaluation research* is a major type of applied research, typically undertaken by social scientists to determine if ongoing social programs are working as they should. Evaluations tend to focus on programs that are ameliorative in nature, such as remedial education, health care delivery systems, welfare reforms, and job training programs. Because these types of programs are ongoing, research to evaluate them usually has a shorter time span than some other forms of applied research, such as organizational research.

The results of an evaluation study, in revealing whether a social program is accomplishing what was intended, can have an immediate impact on social policy and political decisions regarding the program's fate—whether it should be continued or stopped, its budget and personnel increased or cut back, and the like. While it should not be expected that the social problems will be eliminated or solved immediately, policy decisions about programs are made immediately on the basis of research results that appear to justify particular actions (Lynn, 1977). There are exceptions to the immediate application of evaluation results, however, as when findings are contradictory or equivocal. Evaluations of some preschool Head Start programs (intended to educate underprivileged preschoolers so that they will become achieving and self-sufficient adults), income tax maintenance programs, and juvenile delinquency prevention studies have not always agreed about the program's success or failure, thus leading to indecision among planners and decision makers. Immediate action based on evaluations also can be limited when the actual effects of a social program are not readily apparent. The effects of the Cambridge-Somerville Youth Study (discussed in Chapter 1) were not apparent until 30 years later, and policymakers rarely are willing to wait that long for evaluations of social programs. An unfortunate problem with evaluation research is that it does take a short-term perspective, and this "quick fix" attitude increases the likelihood of premature use of evaluation results.

There are a number of vested interests in the design and implementation of evaluation studies, and because their results are likely to affect people's jobs, education, or health, conflicting role expectations can be expected. Like research conducted in organizations, evaluation research raises some unique ethical questions about whose interests are served and whose point of view should be represented during the research process (Kidder & Judd, 1986). Many of these questions tend to emerge as a result of the evaluation's connection with social and political institutions. Ethical dilemmas in this context can be largely understood as a result of the multiple roles that are performed by the researcher as evaluator (Sieber, 1980). Accordingly, Mirvis and Seashore's (1982) role system approach for evaluating organizational research is applicable in this context as well.

It is often difficult for evaluators to separate their research role from their other roles, such as consultant, teacher, or clinician. When these prescribed role responsibilities overlap, no doubt there will be discrepancies (i.e., role conflicts) from which ethical dilemmas will emerge. The evaluation incident presented in Chapter 2 serves as a good illustration of the kinds of conflicts that may be encountered during an evaluation. Elsewhere, Campbell (1969) has described the inevitability of conflicts between evaluation researchers whose careers require them to evaluate other people's programs and program administrators whose careers depend upon implementing successful programs. Campbell offered the suggestion that these conflicts might be circumvented if administrators adopted more of a scientific attitude that focused on the actual effectiveness of their programs, and if researchers limited their evaluations to programs and not people. By clarifying their roles prior to the actual evaluation, a more cooperative researcher/administrator relationship could develop. This recommendation is consistent with Mirvis and Seashore's notions of openly clarifying and resolving conflicts among roles in organizational settings.

To illustrate the variety of ethical and moral problems that can face evaluators in different settings, Johnson (1985) has described two ethical dilemmas that occur when evaluators work within human service agencies, particularly where clients are referrals of a community family court and child welfare system. The first dilemma involves breaching confidentiality to report a client's illegal behavior (child abuse), whereas the second involves difficulties in defining the evaluator's appropriate role as expert witness. Both of these dilemmas concern the legal and moral implications of interventions into the personal life and legal affairs of agency clients who somehow are connected to an evaluation study.

In addressing the first dilemma, Johnson pointed out that it is useful to consider what other professionals do in parallel situations. For example, criminologists who withhold information about criminal offenses committed by their research subjects legally could face prosecution as an "accessory after the fact" for failure to report a crime. However, apart from the legal implications, some criminologists have argued that the professional has a moral obligation to maintain confidentiality when such promises are made to research participants (Wolfgang, 1981). Juvenile delinquency youth workers similarly face the problem of whether or not to report criminal activity. In such situations, most youth workers will compare the relative benefit of reporting this activity to police with the risk imposed on others and the likelihood that the larger progress being made with the gang may be jeopardized.

Therapists within the professions of psychiatry and clinical psychology have dealt through the courts with the issue of breaching confidentiality when a patient presents a serious danger of violence to another. In the case of *Tarasoff v. Regents of the University of California* (1976), the court decision ruled that therapists are obligated to protect the intended victim against such danger. This decision was eventually broadened by the California Supreme Court to include the obligation of reporting information about the potential violence to police. According to Appelbaum (1981), a few lawsuits by patients against their therapist for breach of confidentiality have occurred since the Tarasoff decision, but the reported outcomes are not yet available.

From the ethical side of the reporting dilemma, it appears that many mental health professionals are using the Tarasoff "duty to warn" decision to bring potential victims more closely into the therapeutic relationship (Appelbaum, 1981). The resolution of the reporting dilemma for many therapists is to encourage the potentially dangerous person to consult with a psychiatrist, priest, or counselor, whose proper function is to counsel the person against committing the offense. If counseling does not appear to be a likely deterrent, then the professional is obligated to report the situation to law officials who could take steps to avert the crime. A more formal procedure for dealing with the reporting dilemma is taken by other professionals. Some mental health workers maintain the therapeutic relationship by informing their clients about the limits of confidentiality, and involving them in defining the relationship between the therapist and the referral agency.

On the basis of these different professional approaches to the confidentiality dilemma in applied settings, Johnson concluded that evaluators "must consider the accountability of their activities to the objectives of the program or organization they intend to assist" (p. 48). In his view, it is contradictory for a researcher to utilize methods and procedures that are contrary to the organization's objectives—for example, when an evaluator consciously chooses not to make it a policy to report child abuse in a program designed to prevent child abuse and neglect. (Because statutes mandating the reporting of child abuse or neglect may vary in different states, readers are cautioned to consult their particular state's laws on this issue).

Johnson arrived at a similar conclusion regarding the role of evaluator in expert witness situations. Although he could not find any evidence of researchers' data or testimony having been subpoenaed by a family court, evaluators nevertheless face that possibility daily in their work. Unlike other courts, which recognize *privileged communications*—the legal right of individuals to prevent certain communications from being revealed in court proceedings without their permission—the statutory laws of family courts in some states provide for the abrogation of privileged communications in child abuse and neglect cases. The basic rationale for disallowing privileged communications in family courts is the belief that all relevant evidence should be made available in order for the court to make a decision that represents the "best interests of the child" (National Center on Child Abuse and Neglect, 1978). Thus the possibility remains that an evaluator might be requested to testify and reveal identifiable information, for example, in a family court determination of whether or not a child at risk of abuse or neglect should be ordered to return home. In most cases of this kind, qualitative data collected by the evaluator through interviews or field observation notes generally are admissible as hearsay evidence (Caulfield, 1978). In addition, the evaluator might be asked to present evidence pertaining to the overall effectiveness of a child abuse and neglect treatment program. The implications of providing evidence about a particular social program in a court for interpretation poses an additional ethical problem for the evaluator.

There are no simple solutions to these dilemmas. For example, it is difficult for program evaluators to employ the methodological strategies for disguising the identities of their subjects in this context because of the various roles the evaluators must play in working with a particular agency: program developer, consultant, evaluator, social work practitioner, and community citizen. Ultimately, decision makers must analyze their own or organizational values and commit themselves to courses of action, regardless of professional standards to the contrary (Johnson, 1985).

## UNANTICIPATED CONSEQUENCES: THE "DARK SIDE" OF PREVENTION RESEARCH

Several of the ethical problems pertaining to applied research in prevention have been discussed earlier in this text. Not yet considered, and perhaps among the most serious ethical problems encountered in social research, are those involving the unintended adverse effects of preventive intervention studies. There are several examples of unanticipated consequences resulting from past applied social research efforts in this area, and these serve as stark reminders of the potentially damaging effects of research in applied settings.

In addition to subject labeling effects (see Chapter 2), there are a number of other unforeseen ways in which innovations might harm individuals; it is especially important that the investigator be aware of these unintended consequences and adjust the informed consent procedure accordingly. That preventive research can be potentially damaging to the individuals it is designed to benefit is a danger that can be easily overlooked or minimized. This point has been strongly stated by Lorion (1984, p. 252), who warned of the *iatrogenic* potential (i.e., the possibility that harm may be caused by a professional's diagnosis, manner, or treatment) of preventive interventions:

> To assume (as opposed to demonstrate) that preventive strategies will have positive or, at worst, neutral consequences represents a naive and irresponsible position. It is inconceivable that an intervention which is designed to avoid or limit the impact of a pathological process or to generate heretofore absent inter- or intra-personal competencies could not be recognized as also able to cause negative outcomes.

A clear illustration of this iatrogenic problem was provided by McCord's (1978) follow-up of the Cambridge-Somerville Youth Study (Chapter 1). As a preventive program aimed at delinquent youths, the Cambridge-Somerville experiment revealed how exposure to certain features of preventive treatments can produce subtle psychological and behavioral effects that are ultimately self-defeating for research participants.

Muñoz (1983) has described two subtle issues that help clarify the processes by which unintended effects occur in prevention research. The first is raised by the emphasis on self-control that is implicit in most intervention approaches, that what happens to participants is in large part under their own control. Acceptance of this message is intended to promote self-fulfillment strategies that allow the individual to approach life experiences in healthier and more adaptive ways. The problem here is that at-risk individuals may turn the message of self-control against themselves by reasoning that the difficulties they are experiencing also must be of their own making. Thus high-risk individuals, such as potential drug abusers, juvenile delinquents, and depressives, may attribute the cause of their current problems internally to presumed personal inadequacies.

A second issue described by Muñoz involves the possibility that intervention strategies targeted to alleviate the incidence of conditions known to place people at high risk for psychological problems might serve instead to increase their occurrence. To illustrate this paradox, Muñoz suggests that a program found to be successful in preventing the negative consequences of divorce could make it easier for people to consider divorce. A similar process might operate to cause a concomitant increase in drug and alcohol abuse or premarital sexual relations as individuals become aware of programs capable of preventing the adverse consequences of those behaviors, such as addiction and sexually communicable diseases, respectively. These examples suggest an "enlightenment effect" not unlike that described by Gergen (1973), in which people become resistant to certain psychological influences by learning about them. Enlightenment effects in prevention research could eventually counteract the effectiveness of particular treatment programs.

Unlike the problem of iatrogenic consequences, where a preventive technique actually harms treated subjects, other unintended effects might arise as a consequence of the success of a program in preventing a mental health problem. That is, it could be that the maladaptive processes determined as being at the root of a mental health problem targeted for prevention were serving useful functions as well for the individual. For example, when Cook (1970) successfully reduced prejudice among individuals who were unaware that they were serving as research subjects, he inadvertently may have caused them great difficulties when they returned to their family and friends who were still prejudiced (Diener & Crandall, 1978).

An example of this problem with more relevance to mental health research stems from the finding that depressives tend to agree with a set of "irrational" personal beliefs consistent with what they perceive is necessary to feel good or consider themselves as worthwhile (Muñoz,

1983). Many of these beliefs are part of a traditional culture that values group cohesiveness (versus individualistic pursuits), such as relying on others, considering others' feelings important, and so on. Convincing at-risk depressives to reexamine these beliefs that have been found to be associated with depression might indeed prevent depression, but also might cause other problems of social adjustment. Similarly, the self-control orientation of prevention programs could threaten the traditional power structure in households where a family member—such as the husband in Latino families—traditionally dominates (Muñoz, 1983). An intervention that successfully conveys the self-control message to individuals might then motivate them to demand more power in their households in an attempt to increase control over their own lives. These examples suggest that the reduction or elimination of certain maladaptive behaviors, beliefs, or thinking processes in at-risk individuals could cause subjects to question a way of life or traditional values at the core of shared belief systems in their cultural environments (see Douglas & Wildavsky, 1982). This issue represents a difficult dilemma for researchers, which is tied to the fact that the lives of subjects may be affected by unanticipated aspects of the social contexts from which the subjects were sampled.

To discontinue successful preventive programs because of their potentially damaging side effects, as some might suggest, would not be the appropriate ethical response to these issues. Instead, changing the focus of the intervention represents one way researchers can approach the problem of unanticipated consequences without reducing research on new treatments. For example, rather than concentrating on the prevention of negative outcomes suffered by victims of divorce, Muñoz (1983) has recommended that research could be more reasonably focused on programs that help high-risk couples to achieve more fulfilling marriages or to avoid marriage altogether when there are strong indications that it will fail.

Others have approached the problem of unanticipated consequences by recommending that prevention investigators take more care in considering the importance of timing their interventions. Gersten et al. (1979) and Lorion (1983, 1984) have pointed out that unintended effects can be avoided if intervention research is designed with an appreciation of the developmental history of functional and dysfunctional processes related to mental health. Certain behaviors targeted for prevention often will be identified in both risk and nonrisk populations; however, those behaviors typically will disappear from nondysfunctional individuals. The careful timing of early detection and remediation efforts is required so that preventive efforts will not cause an interruption of these processes and the premature labeling of certain individuals as "at risk" (Lorion, 1983).

A consideration of the potential unanticipated consequences of prevention research highlights the necessity for considerable preparatory work prior to implementation. In short, unintended effects can be avoided or reduced if investigators take care to apply rigorous evaluation methods to the development, implementation, and assessment of the research program, including a careful definition of the problem, specifying of the target population, and timing of the intervention.

## ETHICAL RESPONSIBILITIES
## WHEN THE RESEARCH IS COMPLETED

The problems described in the preceding section clearly illustrate how lives can be adversely affected by the work of applied social and behavioral scientists. In this section, some of the ethical issues that stem from a consideration of the consequences of research will be evaluated, including the uses and misuses of scientific knowledge in applied settings. The intent here is to sharpen the ethical sensibilities of social researchers who assume that their responsibilities cease with the reporting of research.

### Consequences of Application

The accumulation of social and behavioral knowledge is beset with ethical ambiguities that necessitate the presentation of results in a way that promises the least potential for distortion and the greatest opportunity for social gains. Since anything that social researchers learn can be used for ends beyond their control and even against their values, research should be undertaken only after careful consideration of its plausible consequences. Conflicts between intended or unintended applications of knowledge and beneficial objectives can become intensely emotional moral issues, particularly when researchers are not careful in stipulating the limitations and implications of their investigations.

A number of negative effects associated with scientific knowledge can prevent the net potential benefits of research advances from being realized (Reynolds, 1979). In addition, there is the possibility that data collected for scientific purposes could be used to harm individual participants or aggregates of individuals. Of concern here is the use of sensitive and controversial data in a fashion that embarrasses these individuals, threatens or damages their well-being, or limits their freedom in an unjustified or dangerous way.

One indirect effect of scientific knowledge results from its use for the advantage of special interests rather than of humanity in general or from its use to the general detriment of all. As additional means become available to control such undesirable behaviors as child abuse, rape, homicide, racial discrimination, and addiction, the possibility that control could jeopardize human freedom must be recognized. This problem can be especially destructive when scientific knowledge is used by the powerful or elite to control less powerful groups, such as when organizations use research findings to control the activities of their employees. The ethical dilemma of control and human freedom has been discussed at length by Kelman (1965, 1968) and Miller (1969), among others.

An easily overlooked adverse consequence of much research involves the failure to use new practices and procedures with proven beneficial value. There are numerous examples in the social sciences of knowledge that was not put to use simply because policymakers and the lay public were not aware of, or did not understand, research that was potentially useful to them (Caplan, Morrison, & Stambaugh, 1975; Kramer, 1967). As a typical example, one might consider the research on child development and on the effects of various child-rearing techniques that has not been transmitted to parents (see Clarke-Stewart, 1978). It often takes some time before new knowledge with proven benefits is generally accepted. During the interim, the scientifically demonstrated benefits can be substantial (see Rainwater & Yancey, 1967). In much the same way that it may be against the best interests of science not to conduct certain research because of the losses in probable benefits (Rosenthal & Rosnow, 1984), or unethical to avoid publication of certain results because they do not fit the researcher's values or beliefs (Pervin, 1978), the failure to use findings in a positive way could also be regarded as objectionable.

### The Misuse of Scientific Knowledge

There is always the possibility, which can be attributed either to misunderstanding or to incompetence, that scientific knowledge will be misused (Lindblom & Cohen, 1979). To be sure, scientists should not be considered responsible for a misreading or misinterpretation of their work as long as special care has been taken, when publicizing the research, to state conditions pertinent to the usefulness of the research in applied contexts. But stating the conditions of application and urging extreme caution in terms that even lay persons can understand does not always guarantee that research findings will not be improperly used.

Several illustrations of the use and misuse of scientific knowledge can be found in the research on *forensic psychology* (the area of psychology that scientifically studies questions relevant to the legal, judicial, and correctional systems). In forensic research, an extra burden of responsibility is imposed upon those who, because of the complex nature of the subject matter with which they deal, are not experts in every situation that they encounter and about which they must make decisions. One typical procedure in mock jury research, for example, is to bring subjects into the laboratory and have them read or hear a synopsis of a case. Subjects then separately indicate their opinions concerning the guilt or culpability of the defendant and often are asked to assess punishment or award damages. Mock jury simulations more closely simulate actual jury procedures. In mock jury simulations, the minimal requirements are that subjects be brought together in groups, read, hear, or see the proceedings, and deliberate as a jury. The behavioral researcher engaged in these types of mock jury studies bears an extra obligation to be concerned with functional (Bermant et al., 1974) and conceptual (Vidmar, 1979) verisimilitude. *Functional verisimilitude* is concerned with the degree to which models mimic the behavior of actual juries under conditions of similar input. *Conceptual verisimilitude* is concerned with the degree to which a problem under investigation corresponds to the problem as viewed from a legal perspective. Both considerations reflect a concern for the ethics of generalizability—the responsibility of the researcher for indicating the limits of the obtained relationships between variables so that they are not used improperly or misinterpreted.

When one views mock jury research with a concern for the ethics of generalizability, serious implications can arise. Vidmar (1979) and Meehl (1971) have commented on the tendency of psychologists who work in jury simulation research and in the legal context to overgeneralize and to make critical judgments about the legal system without fully understanding the complexity of the issues. Implicit in their arguments is a concern about the methodological consequences of this tendency. Methodological concern is further explicated by Dillehay and Nietzel (1980), who suggest that effects significant in the laboratory can have little or no practical effect in the applied setting. If researchers are ethically responsible for stipulating the conditions that limit the generalizability of their work, then it follows that all mock jury research should contain statements that make clear the degrees of functional and conceptual verisimilitude of the work, whether it is used by a court or not. Researchers could avoid this responsibility by avoiding reference to the legal context if the research does not meet minimum criteria of functional and conceptual verisimilitude.

The majority of mock jury research reports do not make the differences between the experimental methodology and actual court procedure explicit, yet, as Vidmar (1979) has pointed out, these differences can be substantial. For example, the Supreme Court decision upholding the reduction in size for civil juries (*Colgrove v. Battin*, 1973) was based in part on a mock jury study that compared eight 12-person with eight 6-person juries. Three major hypotheses of no significant differences in verdict, time of deliberation, and number of issues discussed by each panel were not rejected. The lack of power of statistical tests when samples are so small was not discussed, and the naive reader was not warned that such results should not be interpreted to mean that differences do not actually exist.

Another example of the inappropriate use of forensic research involves attempts to utilize social science survey and attitude measurement procedures to influence jury decisions through scientific rejection of jurors (Reynolds, 1979; Saks, 1976). In this procedure, prospective jurors are not approached or tampered with in any way; they are merely compared to other individuals whose attitudes and opinions are known. The comparisons are usually of a demographic nature, although personality tests to measure authoritarianism and the like have also been used. Several social scientists have argued that participation in the courtroom during the jury selection phase of a trial is ethical (Fersch, 1980; Nemeth, 1981; Saks, 1976). For example, Saks suggested that social science involvement in trials is ethical because for many years lawyers have tried, albeit ineptly, to select jurors favorable to their clients, and the emergence of an approach that is potentially successful does not suddenly change an ethical goal into an unethical goal.

The involvement of research scientists in the courtroom raises some important questions about situations in which researchers accept an adversary role. In the U.S. legal system, that role is dictated by both statute and custom. Whereas the adversary is bound to be truthful, he or she is equally bound to present the case in the light most favorable to the client. Failure to do so is a breach of the ethics of the legal profession (Freedman, 1975). Researchers who enter the legal (or any other) arena are bound by the ethics of that profession in addition to their own professional standards. Unfortunately, applied scientists often have insufficient ethical guidance for conducting their applied activities. The issues of major ethical concern for jury researchers, for instance, are considered only briefly in the APA's most recent publication on ethics in the criminal system (Monahan, 1980). This is because there are more pressing ethical dilemmas for behavioral scientists in other areas of the criminal justice system.

The paucity of professional guidance is further evidenced by the fact that many of the disciplines in which applied researchers work have no formal code of ethics. For example, there are no clear guidelines for scientific research in forensic areas. Both the American Bar Association and the American Association of Criminology lack explicit ethical codes that address the protection of human subjects and other issues related to research conduct. Both associations, however, do define and prescribe ethical and responsible professional conduct with respect to clients, the public, and professional colleagues, and they both refer to the importance of contributing to the growth of knowledge. Bower and de Gasparis (1978, Appendix A) have compiled brief descriptions of the ethical codes (or noted their absence) in various professional associations and public-interest organizations devoted to the protection of human subjects; as such, this list represents a valuable resource for applied researchers. More recently, a compilation of ethical statements in a wide range of professional fields (along with information on how copies may be obtained) was prepared by the Center for the Study of Ethics in the Professions (1981).

## Responsibilities of the Applied Social Researcher

There is disagreement in the scientific community about the ethical responsibility of social scientists for the use and misuse of scientific discoveries. Although it appears that many social scientists now feel a greater responsibility than in the past to society and humanity for the knowledge they produce, and are becoming increasingly involved in the decision-making process, attribution of responsibility is by no means a mutually perceived, clear-cut issue. Responsibility for the negative effects associated with application of new or existing knowledge, or with the failure to apply such knowledge, can vary with the nature of the effects (Reynolds, 1979). For example, an investigator who withholds potentially beneficial information can reasonably be held morally responsible for any foregone benefits. Of course, this is not necessarily the case if the investigator withholds data pending corroboration by further evidence. In contrast, responsibility for improper application of knowledge that is widely accepted by the scientific community and relevant applied professionals falls primarily on the applied professionals. According to Reynolds (1979), investigators should be considered responsible for the adverse effects of social knowledge in situations where they fail to inform decision makers of known negative consequences that can accompany application or they fail to provide appropriate interpretations of research findings based on data describing specific groups of individuals. The interested reader is advised to consult Reynolds (1979, pp. 371-381) for a comprehensive analysis of other situations in which responsibility should or should not be placed on the originating scientist.

## SUMMARY

Whether their work is theoretical or applied, social researchers cannot always be expected to have the greatest acumen for evaluating and predicting the potential uses of their research. In addition, there is probably not much that a researcher can do to guard against the possibility that findings will sustain a bias within society, as in cases where prejudiced individuals use results that are consistent with their beliefs to support discriminatory policies (Pervin, 1978). A number of mechanisms could be utilized to control or minimize the negative effects of scientific knowledge, although none can guarantee that research findings will not someday have an adverse consequence. Initially, researchers should make the best possible prediction of how their findings will be used, and, when possible, they should select a course of investigation that will help to protect those who are the focus of the research. Disseminating new information to the widest possible audience will reduce the possibility that a powerful group will use the knowledge for its own welfare or to the detriment of a less powerful segment of society. Widespread reporting of research can also prompt society to insulate itself better against possible misuses.

Other abuses in the application of knowledge can be minimized if researchers remain alert against overly hasty conclusions and misinterpretations of research findings and actively work to prevent such conclusions. It may be that some means of early disclosure of research findings are more ethical than others (Bermel, 1985). Some social researchers could assume more of a nonscientific role by writing to legislators and agencies and by communicating the beneficial and also the destructive uses of scientific knowledge to policymakers, the public, and their students (Diener & Crandall, 1978). Finally, scientists can collectively assume responsibility for the knowledge that they generate through scientific and interdisciplinary organizations—such as the American Association for the Advancement of Science—that communicate scientific knowledge to the public and provide forums for discussion of policy-related issues, and through lobbying associations.

## RECOMMENDED READINGS

American Psychological Association. (1975). *Standards for providers of psychological services.* Washington, DC: Author.

Bowie, N. (1982). *Business ethics.* Englewood Cliffs, NJ: Prentice-Hall.

Corey, G., Corey, M. S., & Callanan, P. (1984). *Issues and ethics in the helping professions* (2nd ed.). Belmont, CA: Wadsworth.

Lindblom, C. E., & Cohen, D. (1979). *Usable knowledge: Social science and social problem solving.* New Haven, CT: Yale University Press.

Lowman, R. L. (Ed.). (1985). *Casebook on ethics and standards for the practice of psychology in organizations.* College Park, MD: Society for Industrial and Organizational Psychology.

Wildavsky, A. (1979). *Speaking truth to power: The art and craft of policy analysis.* Boston: Little, Brown.

## CHAPTER EXERCISES

1. Reconsider the exercises for Chapters 4 and 5. How might Mirvis and Seashore's research role system approach be applied in attempts to resolve the ethical dilemmas posed by the case studies?

2. *Case Study*: A researcher was recently funded for research in alcohol abuse. She tested a variety of hypotheses derived from a complex theoretical model in several field settings. She has now been informed from her funding source that it is interested in giving her continued funding for the research provided she directly applies the results to prevent alcohol abuse. When she protests that her results, while promising, still need corroboration and further work to refine the theoretical model and derived hypotheses, she is told that research funds will not be forthcoming. Since most other funding sources have shifted toward immediate application and "results," she fears that if she does not accept the money, she will be cut off from research support.

Should the researcher refuse to accept this funding, knowing that the model is not refined enough to risk application, or should she accept the funding, knowing that if she does not, she risks losing all hope of further support?

# 7

## *Attitudes and Value Commitments*

The role of values and their implications for ethical responsibility, objective review, and vested interests within the professions recently have become topics of considerable attention and debate in the social and behavioral sciences. A growing body of research suggests that individuals systematically differ in the ways they formulate their ethical appraisals of research. As such, perfect consensus regarding the ethical acceptability of a particular investigation cannot be expected. This chapter considers these and related issues, by focusing on ethical decision making and threats to objective peer review of social research. The desirability of bringing to bear on the interpretations of principal research investigators the judgments of others is emphasized, and suggestions for reducing potential biases stemming from individual differences in assessments of the ethical acceptability of research are offered.

### THE ROLE OF VALUES
### IN SOCIAL RESEARCH

A common thread running through most current professional codes of ethics and governmental ethical standards is the recognition that each case involves a somewhat different set of balancing considerations for and against research that raises ethical issues. This cost-benefit approach leads to the suggestion that ethical conflicts and moral dilemmas are inevitable in the conduct of research. In terms of guidance and application, cost-benefit analysis raises a number of problems; its mechanisms must be examined and reexamined, and appreciated in new and different contexts. Adding to the empirical drawbacks of cost-benefit analysis (including problems inherent in attempts to predict and quantify costs and benefits) is the researcher's conflict of interest in the decision-making process. Judgments concerning the positive and negative attributes of a study must be made by the very person who believes the research to be worthwhile, and who has the most to gain from a favorable verdict. This problem is compounded by the fact that researchers' resolutions regarding the question of potential harm are all too often reduced to statements of personal opinion based on their individual views of morality (Schlenker & Forsyth, 1977). As such, an objective assessment of the various ethical and methodological considerations presented in preceding chapters will be threatened to the extent that the approach taken by the scientist reflects his or her attitudes and value commitments.

Questions about values are particularly important in social intervention studies, for example, because the research often represents an attempt to change patterns the scientist believes are potentially damaging to specific individuals and threatening to society in general. One's definition of a problem targeted for change is likely to be a direct reflection of what one believes to be ideal. Values inevitably enter into intervention studies at all stages of the research process, beginning with the decision that there is a social problem and a need for intervention, definition of the problem in terms of its presumed cause and potential solutions, and identification and selection of research participants for targeted change (Warwick & Kelman, 1973). The ethical question that emerges as a result centers on the extent to which a scientist has the right to impose his or her values—to set goals and select methods in an attempt to affect the lives of those who perhaps do not wish to change their behavior and life experiences or are not aware of what happens to themselves in the process (Redlich & Mollica, 1976).

The assumption that variations in personal values, attitudes, temperament, and other individual characteristics might in some way influence social scientists' resolutions of the ethical problems that beset their research, reflects a subjective side to ethical decision making that is consistent with contemporary, general descriptions of scientific behavior. In many social research investigations it is not at all clear that the good outweighs the bad, and the balance one strikes will depend, in part, on a number of psychological and subjective factors. Ethical decisions and moral judgments may be affected by the investigator's cultural and personal characteristics, interests, and values (Diener & Crandall, 1978), and an objective methodology guided by a utilitarian set of ethical standards cannot always overcome the initial biases associated with individual decision making (Frankena, 1973).

## The Subjective Side of Ethical
## Decisions and Moral Judgments

Recently, the conception of science as a "value-free" enterprise has been seriously challenged, and important questions have been raised about the appropriate relationship between scientific inquiry, objectivity, and the role of scientists' values and beliefs (e.g., Fischer, 1980). Assumptions underlying this value-free view of science have with increasing regularity been criticized as problematic (see Holton, 1973; Koch, 1981; Polanyi, 1958). A number of persons have examined the value/belief systems of scientists for their social implications in areas such as social policy, politics, economics, and styles and quality of life (e.g., Bazelon, 1982; Kiesler, 1980; Krasner & Houts, 1984; Sarason, 1978, 1981). As a result, these analyses have begun to lift the veil of value neutrality that for so long surrounded the scientific disciplines (Krasner & Houts, 1984).

A traditional view of science was that the only values supposed to influence research were the scientific values placed on truth and objective methodology (Weber, 1949). This view prescribed complete detachment of personal values from scientific research. Associated with this depiction of science, the public image of scientists almost always emphasized the objectivity of their work, and their cool, detached, impassive, and dispassionate observation of phenomena that had no emotional meaning for them (Roe, 1961). However, Merton (1973), Mitroff (1974), Mahoney (1976), and others have critically examined the prevalent stereotyped image of the scientist as a paragon of objectivity and passionless purveyor of the truth, and have documented scientific behavior that presents a quite different characterization.

Mitroff (1974) conducted a series of extensive interviews with eminent geoscientists who had publicly committed themselves to various lunar hypotheses prior to the Apollo missions to the moon. His research clearly showed that the scientist-subjects were often prejudiced and dogmatic when the Apollo findings were made known, refusing to alter their beliefs and eager to discredit data that contradicted their hypotheses. In fact, the group of geoscientists themselves were unanimously in agreement that the notion of the objective, emotionally disinterested scientist was naive. In defending the role of emotionalism and passionate devotion in science, Mitroff has argued that scientists' feelings motivate their queries and facilitate perseverance. In his opinion, discovery in science is intimately bound to the strong psychological emotions and intense commitments that sustain the process of scientific inquiry.

Reflecting on Mitroff's views, Mahoney (1976) has speculated that a researcher's feelings are applauded so long as they stem from intellectual incentives, such as curiosity and a thirst for knowledge. By contrast, Mahoney's critique of the stereotyped image of scientists primarily focused on a set of characteristics that might be traced to psychosocial, rather than intellectual, incentives. These characteristics present a picture of the researcher as "often a selfish, ambitious, and petulant defender of personal recognition and territoriality" who, in his or her experimental research, is often selective, expedient, and not immune to distorting data (Mahoney, 1976, p. 6).

According to Mahoney, the often neglected emotions that can be traced to psychosocial motives may stimulate some of the least admirable behaviors in researchers. For example, the quest for personal recognition (often described as a consequence of a "priority race" in science) might at times be associated with hasty research and publication as well as with experimental and conceptual risk taking. Also, personal motives somehow might influence scientists to look selectively for and accept data that support their viewpoints and to ignore or discredit data that do not. Peer recognition perhaps leads to a dangerous self-complacency that threatens prior caution and self-examination, and that makes these undesirable consequences all the more likely (Cole & Cole, 1973).

Scientific behavior characterized by subjectivity and emotionalism has serious implications for ethical decision making and moral judgments. Emotionally involved and committed to their research for personal gain and the advancement of knowledge, researchers may wittingly or unwittingly conduct research with questionable ethics. Intense commitment to a study means that the investigator will often be an unlikely source of an objective ethical analysis (Diener & Crandall, 1978). Many scientists are apt to overrate the importance of their work and underestimate potential harms as they move closer to a decision to proceed with a proposed study. Of course, it is likely that the direction and extent to which subjective factors influence individual cost-benefit assessments and other ethical decisions vary greatly among researchers.

## Research on Ethical Decision Making

Studies pertaining to ethical decision making and attitudes toward social and behavioral research suggest that certain extrascientific characteristics of researchers may be associated with differential stances on ethical issues, or influence the kinds of ethical decisions drawn. For example, despite the paucity of research on the factors that affect moral judgments, some recent work suggests that ethical issues in psychological research are intimately tied to the more general moral positions held by psychologists. Schlenker and Forsyth (1977) examined the degree to which judgments of the ethical acceptability of two controversial experiments that investigated obedience to authority were affected by ethical ideology. Student subjects read a description of the general procedure and results of either Milgram's obedience experiment (in which subjects were ordered to deliver "electric shocks" to an innocent victim) or West, Gunn, and Chernicky's 1975 field experiment (in which subjects were asked to participate in a Watergate-like burglary). Subjects then were asked to judge the ethical acceptability of the experiment by responding to a series of questions about it. Each subject additionally completed an ethics positions questionnaire designed to assess individual differences in moral philosophy. In part, the findings revealed that a judge's ideology determined how the perceived benefits and costs of the research were correlated with moral judgments. *Teleologists* (those who rely on the consequences of an action to judge its morality) weighted scientific benefits heavily; *deontologists* (those who base their ethical judgments on universal moral rules without exception) weighted participants' costs heavily; and *skeptics* (those who reject specific ethical principles and assume that inviolate moral codes cannot be formulated) weighted both heavily.

Schlenker and Forsyth theorized that people differ in (1) their evaluations of the quality and importance of consequences and (2) their reliance on universal rules of ethics when making moral judgments. Two bipolar factors emerged from their subjects' questionnaire responses to a number of items related to moral judgments of psychological research, the first corresponding to perspective with regard to consequences (idealism versus pragmatism) and the second to emphasis on universal moral principles (relativism versus rule-deontologism). These two dimensions yield a 2 × 2 classification system of ethical ideologies and indicate that individuals may adopt one of four different approaches to making ethical judgments, depending on whether or not they advocate idealistic or pragmatic values and believe moral judgments are universal or relative (Forsyth, 1980). Forsyth (1980) has reported further success using the ethical positions classification system to predict differences in subjects' judgments of others' morality (e.g., those who endorsed different ethical ideologies significantly differed in the emphasis of good and bad consequences, overall severity of moral judgment, and their openness to justification).

There are other similar indications that researchers systematically differ in the ways they interpret or resolve ethical questions. West and Gunn (1978) have argued that there is a fundamental difference in the perception of human nature on the part of humanistically oriented psychologists and experimental social psychologists in assessing the long-term effects of experimental deception. In contrast to the humanists, the experimental social psychologists seem to view the effects of deception as short-term and transitory. This suggests that the effects stemming from the ethical positions of behavioral scientists may extend to the methodology and epistemology to which a researcher is committed for scientific gain (see Krasner & Houts, 1984; Miller, 1972; Sieber, 1982a). Humanistic critics of deception tend to favor role-play methodologies, in which the experimenter and the subject are engaged in a collaborative effort as "co-investigators." Traditional experimentalists usually prefer a clear distinction between experimenter and subjects, and they tend to view role-play designs as lacking generalizability beyond the research setting. Sieber (1982a) has suggested that while humanistically oriented researchers and deterministically oriented researchers are likely to encounter different ethical dilemmas in their social research, a blending of the deterministic and humanistic approaches may be necessary to solve the dilemmas.

In their research on individual differences in ethical decision making, Hamsher and Reznikoff (1967) systematically assessed the attitudes and feelings of a sample of Connecticut psychologists with regard to five ethical issues in research and graduate training: (1) experimental use of stress, (2) emphasis on ethics in graduate training, (3) external control over research, (4) relative importance of ethics, and (5) emphasis on subject consent. Their analyses focused on how psychologists felt about the ethical issues raised and what aspects of their situations and backgrounds were reflected in differential responding. The study represents an empirical determination of the discrepancies between psychologists' values and their practice. In general, those not conducting any research at all placed considerable emphasis on the ethical issues, while those doing nothing but research evidenced relative unconcern. For example, an inverse correlation was obtained for percentage of time devoted to research and disapproval of the use of stress in psychological experiments. Only those psychologists with little or no involvement with research viewed stress conditions as ethically questionable. In addition, women showed greater concern than men for the ethical issues.

Hamsher and Reznikoff also reported that full-time investigators opposed external regulations much more strongly than did the other respondents. This finding is somewhat consistent with survey data more recently obtained by the Department of Health and Human Services (DHEW, 1978) on the effectiveness of IRBs. Included in the survey was a comparison of the attitudes of behavioral and social scientists and review committee members toward review procedures and committees. The operation of the review process was viewed more favorably than unfavorably by most investigators and board members on questions referring to protection of the rights and welfare of human subjects, improvement of the quality of scientific research, and the efficiency of the review procedure at their institutions. However, a substantial minority of researchers, as opposed to board members, felt that the review procedure is an unwarranted intrusion of the investigator's autonomy and that a typical review committee, at least to some extent, gets into areas that are inappropriate to the IRB's function, makes some judgments that it is not qualified to make, and impedes the progress of research.

It may very well be, as Hamsher and Reznikoff (p. 204) conjectured, that the inverse relationship between a researcher's experience and his or her interest in ethical problems "may reflect the greater simplification of issues by the uninvolved, or it may be due to a 'hard-headed' scientism of researchers." But it also may be that behavioral scientists strongly committed to research view ethical strictures as potential barriers to their own scientific progress and academic freedom.

In a replication and extension of Hamsher and Reznikoff's study, Kimmel (1983) surveyed 259 American psychologists in an attempt to determine the degree to which ethical decisions involving cost-benefit assessments can be predicted from background information about the evaluator. It was expected that some of the biosocial and professional attributes of American psychologists would be significant predictors of their ethical judgments. Among the individual difference variables considered were demographic characteristics (sex, age), biographical characteristics related to training (highest degree attained, area of the degree, and number of years since receiving the degree), and character-istics reflecting professional experience and employment (licensure status, major field/speciality, academic rank, nature of employment, time spent in various employment activities, and nature and history of affiliation with the American Psychological Association). Respondents evaluated the ethical acceptability of 18 hypothetical examples of behavioral research varying in levels of cost and benefit. The analyses revealed that certain background characteristics were more important than others in predicting evaluations of the ethical acceptability of research. Psychologists who tended to be more approving in their ethical evaluations (thereby suggesting a greater emphasis on research benefits) were those who (a) were males, (b) had held their highest degree for a longer period of time, (c) had received the degree in a basic psychology area (such as social, experimental, or developmental psychology), and (d) were employed in research-oriented contexts. Psychologists who tended to disapprove or reflect conservatism in their judgments (thereby suggesting a greater emphasis on research costs) were those who (a) were females, (b) had held their highest degree for a shorter period of time, (c) had received the degree in an applied psychology area (such as counseling, school, or community psychology), and (d) were employed in service-oriented contexts.

The tendency for female and service-oriented psychologists to be less approving than others in their ethical assessments might be explained by their greater sensitivity to the needs of others. For example, they may have perceived subjects in the evaluated situations as potential "victims" of research. These evaluators also might have held science in general, and behavioral research in particular, in somewhat lower regard than male and research-oriented psychologists. On the other hand, psychologists employed in research-oriented contexts no doubt have considerable faith in the potential merits of scientific research, perceive research psychologists as engaged in a worthy enterprise, and may recognize that their research does not cause obvious harm. Their devotion to the goals and processes of behavioral research could account, in part, for their emphasis on research benefits. A similar interpretation could explain the finding that revealed general area of highest academic degree as an important predictor of ethical decisions. The tendency for psychologists who received their highest degree in a fundamental psychology area to be more approving in their judgments than those who received a degree in an applied psychology area might be traced to the professional and scientific values that were shaped during the training experiences of these psychologists. Those trained in fundamental areas no doubt are more likely to adhere to a view that behavioral research is, by nature, ethical and value-free, thus leading them to underestimate potentially adverse research consequences. However, those with applied training backgrounds perhaps are more apt to disapprove of research that does not appear to be beneficial to the research participants with whom they might identify. Finally, the tendency for approval in senior psychologists' evaluations of research could be explained by their apparent hesitancy to judge others' research strictly because of a sensitivity to the methodological difficulties in conducting human research while maintaining a strict adherence to ethical regulations. Junior evaluators, by contrast, are likely to experience conflicts or uncertainties in their ethical judgments, which they might compensate for with increased vigilance and conservatism in their decisions.

Taken together, the research on ethical decision making demonstrates that individuals systematically differ in the ways they formulate their ethical appraisals of research, and that perfect consensus regarding the ethical acceptability of a particular investigation cannot be expected. Given that individuals tend to differ in their ethical judgments of research involving more than minimal risk, a decision to dispense with the services of certain types of evaluators on ethics committees and the like would probably not be the most appropriate option in the long run. Although social scientists have become more enlightened about the ethical dilemmas inherent in human subject research, the tendencies for male and research-oriented evaluators to be more approving of research, and female and service-oriented evaluators to be less approving, have remained largely unchanged. This finding is somewhat contrary to the expectation than an increased sensitivity to the rights of research subjects and past abuses in science would have created a conservative shift among decision makers (see Chapter 8). It also reflects a lack of ethical consensus in the social sciences (see Atwell, 1981; Holden, 1979).

## IMPLICATIONS FOR PEER REVIEW

In light of the research reviewed in the preceding section, it is not surprising that substantial inconsistency has been found in the application of ethical and methodological standards among institutional review boards in decisions to approve or disapprove research, and in reasons for or against approval. For example, Eaton (1983) found that experienced reviewers were in agreement about the appropriateness (for their treatment of human subjects) of 111 psychological research proposals only 8% of the time over a ten-month period. Reviewers in Eaton's study, however, did not make up actual review committees but were other members of the psychology department in which the proposals were prepared. In a study using actual human subject review committees, Goldman and Katz (1982) investigated the adequacy of peer review among 22 IRBs at major universities with medical colleges. The IRBs were asked to review three medical research protocols and consent forms according to their standard procedures and to explain their decisions. Each of the three projects posed serious ethical issues, including flaws in the research design and a consent form that was incomplete and in violation of federal guidelines. It was expected that different IRBs would reach similar judgments on identical protocols and would apply the same standards to each. The results, however, revealed that while there was consistency among the IRBs in their nonapproval of the three projects reviewed, there was substantial inconsistency in (1) the reasons offered in support of similar decisions and (2) application of ethical, methodological, and informed consent standards.

Methodological objections tended to be raised by most of the 22 boards, but only 9 required modifications in design or disapproved the project on ethical grounds. The intentional methodological flaw—involving the risk that the treatment and control groups in the original protocol would lack comparability due to inadequate randomization of patients—remained largely undetected. (Consideration of aspects of a proposed study's methodology represents an important component of a review board's cost-benefit judgment. A poorly designed study is not likely to accrue any scientific contribution and therefore could not offset even the most minor costs to subjects. Under present and past DHHS guidelines, IRBs are permitted to engage in scientific review of proposed studies.)

While most of the boards found problems in the consent form, their objections and responses seemed to defy any pattern. Some of the boards requested greater specification of the actual procedures for administering the treatment and measuring effects, while others sought clarification of confidentiality procedures, more complete explanation of potential benefits and risks, or a more explicit comparison of alternative medical treatments. Other differences were apparent in the specific ethical and methodological objections to each of the three medical protocols, further demonstrating that the IRBs responded in dissimilar ways to identical research proposals. In short, variations were apparent in their evaluations of ethical problems, and a substantial number of review boards approved unacceptable research designs.

Although it appears from Goldman and Katz's results that IRBs are overly lenient in their decisions involving methodologically flawed and ethically problematic studies, other investigations of peer review suggest the contrary. Smith and Berard (1982) found that in spite of apparent variations between review committees, IRB members may be more cautious overall than either investigators or prospective subjects. In their study, student subjects assumed the role of IRB members and evaluated the appropriateness of Asch's (1955) classic study of conformity in which subjects were deceived. Students tended to make more restrictive judgments as review board members than when they were asked to assume the role of participants in the study. Similarly, Sullivan and Deiker (1973) and Rugg (1975) found that college students, the very population most commonly tapped to be research participants in psychological experiments, were generally less strict about the ethical acceptability of experimental procedures (e.g., involving stress, physical pain, danger, or a threat to their self-esteem) than were professional psychologists.

In a recent investigation of the role of personal values in review board decisions, Ceci, Peters, and Plotkin (1985) had 157 university IRBs review hypothetical proposals that were identical in their treatment of research participants but were different in their degree of social sensitivity and their level of ethical concerns. Nine sample research proposals describing an investigation of hiring discrimination were developed. The proposals were characterized by one of three levels of ethical problems (the use of deception; the use of deception plus a failure to debrief subjects following their participation; and no technical violations, according to the 1981 DHHS guidelines) within each of three levels of social sensitivity. Level of social sensitivity was varied by including proposals to examine discrimination against minorities and women in corporate hiring practices, proposals for documenting reverse discrimination against white males in corporate hiring, and nonsensitive proposals studying discrimination in the hiring of obese and short individuals (with no mention of race or sex).

Each IRB randomly received one of the proposals and was asked to provide a normal review and decision, along with narrative comments describing their deliberations. It was found that socially sensitive proposals were twice as likely as nonsensitive proposals to be rejected by the review committees. Outcomes for socially sensitive proposals apparently were not influenced by the presence or absence of ethical problems, since sensitive proposals were as likely to be rejected whether or not they contained deception of debriefing violations. The foremost reason given for nonapproval of sensitive proposals that involved ethical concerns, such as the use of deception, tended to be the violation itself (i.e., deception). The most frequent reason given for nonapproval of sensitive proposals not involving ethical concerns was methodological, such as a poorly selected control group. This tendency for sensitive proposals to be disapproved even though they did not include ethically problematic procedures was interpreted by Ceci et al. as an indication that the IRBs used whatever reasons were most convenient to justify their nonapproval of the socially objectionable studies.

Based on these findings, Ceci et al. concluded that the sociopolitical ideologies of IRB members appear to play a critical role in the review decisions involving socially sensitive research proposals. Contrary to federal mandate, the sociopolitical consequences of the proposed research (e.g., the discrediting of Affirmative Action policies) seemed to enter into reviewers' ethical analyses. Because the same type of proposal involving the same level of violation often was approved at one institution but not at another in their study, Ceci et al. suggested that luck might sometimes be involved in the approval of a research proposal, especially one that is socially sensitive. That is, a favorable decision might simply be a matter of where one happened to be working when the proposal was submitted for review. The reason for this probably is related to institutional differences, such as the makeup of reviewers (e.g., whether they represent theoretical or clinical departments, natural or social sciences, and the like), university policies reactive to federal or state mandates, or broad religious doctrines.

Institutional review boards originally were established in the policy and regulation of the U.S. Department of Health and Human Services to ensure that researchers would consider the interests of human subjects as an important and formal stage of social science research. Although variations can be expected among IRBs (e.g., as a consequence of differences in community values), consistency is essential in confirming their ability to achieve their goals in the review process. But the internal inconsistencies that appear to characterize many ethical review committees indicate that a comprehensive model for assessing the adequacy of human research has yet to be adopted (Goldman & Katz, 1982).

Some individuals have argued that reliability in ethics reviews is neither inherently desirable nor worth striving for. For example, Doob (1983) believes that IRBs should provide a forum for their members, as representatives of different community values, to present a diversity of opinions about the acceptability of human research. According to Doob, high levels of agreement among review board members are not desirable, in that they "reflect an inadequate sampling of views" (p. 269). This view, however, may not serve the best interests of the researcher or society, as when a proposal is rejected or modified because of the concerns of a few overly cautious or biased IRB members (Ceci et al., 1985).

Although most social scientists appear to accept the concept of peer review in principle, there appears to be a growing dissatisfaction with the review process in actual practice (Ceci et al., 1985). In addition to the problems of variability, unreliability, and the role played by reviewers' values, critics of the IRB process have questioned its increasingly bureaucratic nature (Pattullo, 1980), costliness (Cohen, 1982), and effects on researchers' choice of topics (Glynn, 1978). As social scientists continue to view the review procedure with suspicion and hostility, conflicts between researchers and IRBs will result, even when all parties involved are working toward the common goal of protecting subject interests. It thus is apparent that in order for peer review to ensure a level of protection that otherwise would be absent, a mutually reinforcing relationship between investigators and IRB members must be established. For this to occur, responsibility in improving the communication aspects of the review process must be shared by all decision makers involved. Members of review committees could clarify unclear guidelines and keep investigators fully informed of unfamiliar regulations. In turn, by providing adequate information about risks to subjects in a study seeking potentially sensitive information, investigators could avoid a subsequent conflict with an IRB forced to request additional information.

Tanke and Tanke (1982) have recommended several methods that can be used by IRB members and investigators to minimize the problems of communication between them. For example, IRBs can prepare their members for the review process through training sessions, communication with other IRBs, and solicitation and application of research results relevant to ethical decision making. Similarly, investigators can aid the review process by familiarizing themselves with current ethical standards and principles of review, incorporating ethics into their research designs, and by undertaking research in areas related to subjects' interests. In fact, this educational function of the institutional review process may be more effective than its current regulatory function in serving society and human research participants through social science research (Tanke & Tanke, 1982).

## SUMMARY

Given that individuals systematically differ in the ways they formulate their ethical appraisals of research, perfect consensus regarding the ethicality of a particular investigation cannot be expected. However, if the relative importance of the many factors that influence judgments pertinent to ethical decision making can be enumerated, clarified, and weighed in subsequent research—on topics such as the influence of individual personality differences, the impact of early experience and socialization, moral ideology, the subject matter and content of evaluated research, the impact of institutional values on review board members, and so on—social researchers may then be able to deal effectively with their ethical dilemmas and obtain a fuller understanding of their differences through reasoned and informed discussion.

## RECOMMENDED READINGS

Cooke, R. A., Tannenbaum, A. S., & Gray, B. (1977). A survey of institutional review boards and research involving human subjects. Appendix to *Report and recommendations: Institutional review boards.* Washington, DC: The National Commission for the Protection of Human Subjects of Biomedical and Behavioral Research, U.S. Department of Health, Education, and Welfare.

Lowrance, W. W. (1985). *Modern science and human values.* New York: Oxford.

Mahoney, M. J. (1976). *Scientist as subject: The psychological imperative.* Cambridge, MA: Ballinger.

Merton, R. K. (1973). *The sociology of science: Theoretical and empirical investigations.* Chicago: University of Chicago Press.

Tanke, E. D. & Tanke, T. J. (1982). Regulation and education: The role of the institutional review board in social science research. In J. E. Sieber (Ed.), *The ethics of social research: Fieldwork, regulation, and publication.* New York: Springer-Verlag.

## CHAPTER EXERCISES

1. Find an example of a research study in your field that raises ethical issues. Write a brief summary of the study and present it for review to a group consisting of four other individuals, each of whom also summarized a study. In the role of an institutional review board, would the group have approved or disapproved of the studies, or have recommended modifications in their design or procedure? Be able to defend your decisions.

2. Write a brief essay describing your attitude about the current institutional review process. Do you believe that IRBs are necessary, or do they represent a serious impediment to progress in the social sciences?

# 8

## *Conclusion and Recommendations*

One of the primary objectives of this text has been to raise the ethical sensibility of those individuals who assume the role of applied social researcher—to help clarify the range of ethical problems that might be encountered in that role and some approaches that might be used in thinking about proper courses of action. A number of specific methodological suggestions have been incorporated throughout the preceding chapters in hopes that the many difficulties that arise during the social research process can be dealt with in an efficient and objective fashion, or else avoided altogether. Towards these same ends, this chapter provides some general recommendations for future ethical progress in applied social research.

Ethical decision making is neither a perfectly rational nor entirely timeless enterprise, and even after a considered judgment about the issues involved in a given situation has been made, doubts about whether or not one's subsequent behavior was ethical may remain. Jerrell and Jerrell (1985, p. 73) have likened the moral and ethical grounds inherent in evaluation research to a terrain "plagued with expanses of quicksand at every turn," although a researcher's journey can be made considerably safer by "keeping a good road map handy and watching for road signs" along the way. This analogy seems to apply not only to evaluation research but to all other forms of social research as well. Of course, even if it were possible to erect directional or warning signs to assist researchers in their ethical choices, such signs would not be entirely adequate for resolving specific dilemmas, which by their very nature are complex, differentiated, and likely to stem from competing values.

As we continue to proceed with social research in applied settings, we can expect a growing wealth of documentation on the conditions under which certain interventions are successful in reducing certain social problems (or otherwise improving the human condition) and on what side effects might be anticipated as a result of their implementation. Without conducting the appropriate studies it may never be possible to determine whether an intervention is helpful.

In conclusion, the following five recommendations are offered for guiding the future of ethical social research in applied settings:

(1) *Research subjects should be considered as another "granting institution," granting us their valuable time in return for our generation of valuable scientific knowledge.* To proceed ethically, it is important for social researchers to bear in mind that their first obligation is to those persons who cooperate with and participate in the research process, and that it is their interests that first must be considered during the preparatory stages of program development. Many of the problems that arise when researchers impose their frames of reference on behavior can be avoided when subjects are treated as partners in the research enterprise. This recommendation argues for a more balanced relationship between investigator and research participants than is typically found in social research. Thus it is essential that investigators seek input from a variety of sources in society prior to and during formulation of a social research program, particularly those who will be most directly affected by the research. Broadening one's perspective in this way should lead to the development of social programs that do not solely reflect the values and goals of the scientist or the most powerful segments of society, and is likely to reduce the possibility that researchers will choose only programs that already are politically endorsed.

By adopting the goals and strategies selected and preferred by the politically powerful in society, researchers stand to benefit from the shared advocacy that is likely to follow, but there may be costs involved that cannot be reliably predicted. For example, there are some who have argued that mental health programs can potentially operate as an arm of the political system in helping people adjust to unjust conditions and by emphasizing what the individual can do for him or herself (Muñoz, 1983). Certain intervention techniques might not have an impact in particular segments of the population, such as groups that might better be served by focusing on social, economic, and physical health issues for those in need. A research approach that emphasizes how elderly, sick, and poor individuals think and behave thus may be misdirected, and turn out to be a waste of resources not in the best interests of these target groups.

(2) *The traditional cost-benefit model that underlies ethical decision making in social research should be modified to emphasize (a) the outcomes of both doing AND not doing the research, and (b) the*

*possibilities of doing the research in another manner.* Rosenthal and Rosnow (1984) recently have described the inadequacy of the traditional decision model typically used by researchers in their cost-benefit analyses. While this model includes the costs (potential harm to subjects, time, expenditures of money, and so on) and benefits (to subjects, to others at different times and places, to the investigator, and so on) of doing the research, it fails to consider the costs and benefits of *not* doing the study. As diagrammed in Figure 8.1, the decision is made to carry out studies falling at D, and to not carry out studies at A. Studies falling at B-C are those most likely to lead to indecision.

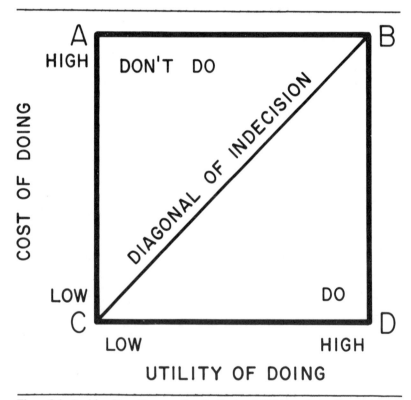

Figure 8.1   Decision Plane Representing the Cost and Utility ot Doing Research

SOURCE: Rosenthal, R., & Rosnow, R. L. (1984). Applying Hamlet's question to the ethical conduct of research: A conceptual addendum. *American Psychologist*, Vol. 39, p. 562. Copyright 1984 by the American Psychological Association. Reprinted by permission of the publisher and author.

Rosenthal and Rosnow recommend that the conceptual model for doing research be combined with a similar model for not doing research (Figure 8.2) in order to provide a more complete analysis of the outcomes of *doing* and *not doing* a study. The result is a third two-dimensional decision square (Figure 8.3) that is formed by the decision diagonals of Figure 8.1 and Figure 8.2. Points near D indicate that the study should be done, while points near D' indicate that the study should not be done. According to Rosenthal and Rosnow (p. 562), the conceptual modification should "improve our thinking about issues of cost and utility by pointing out graphically that there are clearly two sides to be fully considered in terms of the ethics of whether to undertake

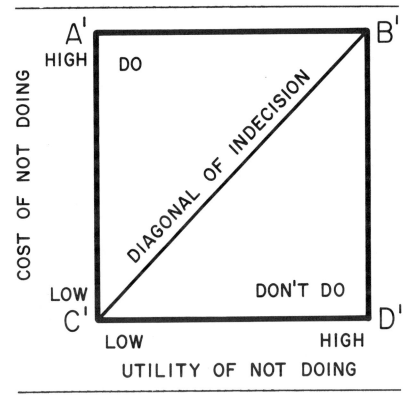

Figure 8.2 Decision Plane Representing the Cost and Utility of Not Doing Research

SOURCE: Rosenthal, R., & Rosnow, R. L. (1984). Applying Hamlet's question to the ethical conduct of research: A conceptual addendum. *American Psychologist*, Vol. 39, p. 562. Copyright 1984 by the American Psychological Association. Reprinted by permission of the publisher and author.

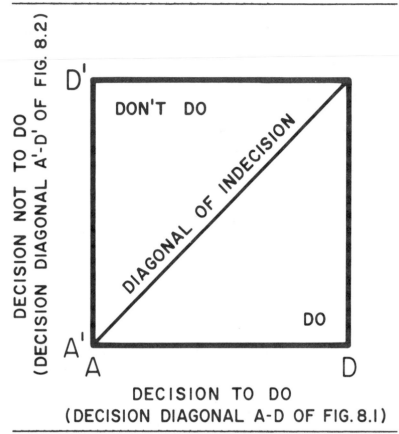

Figure 8.3  Composite Plane Representing the Decisions "to Do" and "Not to Do" Research

SOURCE: Rosenthal, R., & Rosnow, R. L. (1984). Applying Hamlet's question to the ethical conduct of research: A conceptual addendum. *American Psychologist*, Vol. 39, p. 562. Copyright 1984 by the American Psychological Association. Reprinted by permission of the publisher and author.

a given research study."

While useful in pointing out the ethical implications of not conducting research, it should be noted that Rosenthal and Rosnow's model is a simplistic one that is only meant to tell part of the story when it comes to actual decision-making situations. Perhaps a more basic inadequacy of the traditional decision model is that it implies that benefits and costs can be measured and weighted using objectively assigned numeric values. Instead, researchers are more likely dealing with bands of uncertainty when considering whether a study should or should not be conducted, of which several dimensions may be comparable. It also can be argued that the appropriate question for researchers may not be the all-or-none one, between doing and not doing the research, but between doing the research in this way and using the same resources (time, energy, money, and so on) to do a different research project. On a practical level, most research questions can be pursued in more than one manner and, as such, the ethically acceptable decision would be to act in a way that is most likely to lead to a preponderance of good over bad consequences. This poses a challenge to researchers to use their creativity and methodological skills to devise innovative methods that preserve both scientific validity and morality.

(3) *A more detailed reporting of ethical procedures used should be required and expected in all published social research.* One means by which current and future researchers can become better educated about ethical procedures is through the reporting of ethical practices in published research. However, there are indications that such reporting practices are not nearly as widespread as they could be. For example, Adair and Lindsay (1983) found that 81% of the authors of empirical research that appeared in the *Journal of Personality and Social Psychology* during 1979 claimed they had used some form of debriefing in their studies; however, debriefing was reported in less than half of their published articles. Although reports of subject debriefing generally have increased in published empirical articles over the past three decades, few researchers describe (or else journal editors leave out) what subjects are told about the experiment or the form in which that information is presented (Adair, Dushenko, & Lindsay, 1985). With the exception of Mills's (1976) and Sieber's (1983) detailed recommendations for debriefing subjects when deception is used, very little has been written about how and when debriefing should be presented (Adair, Lindsay, & Carlopio, 1983). More detailed journal reporting of the components and techniques of ethical research practices could help to set standards that would be instructive for future researchers.

(4) *A focus on the ethical acceptability of applied research should become a critical component of a mutually reinforcing applied scientific community.* When the applied social science movement got underway, it was widely believed that one well-trained and honest researcher (or team) producing one research report resulted in a valid scientific solution to a given problem. Campbell and Kimmel (1985) have argued, consistent with the modern theory of science espoused by Merton (1973), Polanyi (1958, 1966, 1969), and Ravetz (1971), among others, that the validity of scientific truth claims comes not from the innate or indoctrinated honesty and competence of a single scientist, but rather from a mutually reinforcing (i.e., rewarding and disciplining) scientific

community. In this view, valid, ethical research evolves out of competitive replication and criticism, and from a competition for discovery and eminence so organized as to be disclosing (rather than covering-up) of chance error, incompetence, and fraud. A mutually monitoring scholarly community that stays in close communication on shared scientific questions and issues, while still vigorously criticizing one another, is an idea similar to what Merton (1973) has spoken of as the "organized skepticism" of science. From this perspective, the creation of such a social system in the applied science community could represent a move toward promoting a healthy competitive atmosphere for valid research discovery that, at the same time, continues to press for and encourage ethical progress and practice.

(5) *Evaluations of the ethical acceptability of social research require an awareness of the ethical climate in society and in the scientific community.* It has been argued that a philosophical shift in scientists' ethical viewpoints appears to have occurred during the 1970s (Holden, 1979). During the 1960s, the predominant ethical philosophy in the sciences seems to have been one characterized by a concern for human well-being in general and a concomitant emphasis on utilitarian cost-benefit equations. The 1970s may have marked the beginning of a pendulum swing back to a more conservative position, emphasizing ethical judgments based on universal rules. This shift in ethical context could be considered a result of an increased concern in American society for the basic rights of individuals and an awareness among scientists of abuses of the human rights of participants in social research and in other scientific activities (Atwell, 1981). This suggests the importance of adding a time dimension to the framework of future decision-making models.

## SUMMARY

According to some individuals, a conservative stance is developing toward social research applications as a result of a growing concern about the costs of unsuccessful and premature interventions (see Lorion, 1984). If this growing conservatism represents a threat to objective ethical assessments among those decision makers who must determine whether to proceed or abandon research, then the resulting decisions *not* to do the research are discouraging. If instead the trend means that social researchers are becoming more sensitive to the issues described in this book, it is by all means an encouraging sign for future social research endeavors.

# REFERENCES

Adair, J. G., Dushenko, T. W., & Lindsay, R.C.L. (1985). Ethical regulations and their impact on research practice. *American Psychologist, 40*, 59-72.

Adair, J. G., & Lindsay, R.C.L. (1983). *Debriefing subjects: A comparison of published reports with a self-report survey.* Unpublished manuscript, University of Manitoba, Winnipeg, Canada.

Adair, J. G., Lindsay, R.C.L., & Carlopio, J. (1983). Social artifact research and ethical regulations: Their impact on the teaching of experimental methods in psychology. *Teaching of Psychology, 10*, 159-162.

Adams, K. A. (1985). Gamesmanship for internal evaluators: Knowing when to "hold 'em" and when to "fold 'em." *Evaluation and Program Planning, 8*, 53-57.

American Psychological Association. (1953). *Ethical standards of psychologists.* Washington, DC: Author.

American Psychological Association. (1974). *Standards for educational and psychological tests.* Washington, DC: Author.

American Psychological Association. (1977). *Standards for providers of psychological services* (rev. ed.). Washington, DC: Author.

American Psychological Association. (1981a). *Ethical principles of psychologists.* Washington, DC: Author.

American Psychological Association. (1981b). Specialty guidelines for the delivery of services by industrial/organizational psychologists. *American Psychologist, 36*, 664-669.

American Psychological Association. (1982). *Ethical principles in the conduct of research with human participants.* Washington, DC: Author.

American Sociological Association. (1971). *Code of ethics.* Washington, DC: Author.

Angell, R. C. (1967). The ethical problems of applied sociology. In P. F. Lazarsfeld, W. H. Sewell, & H. L. Wilensky (Eds.), *The uses of sociology.* New York: Basic Books.

Appelbaum, P. S. (1981). Tarasoff: An update on the duty to warn. *Hospital and Community Psychiatry, 32*, 14-15.

Argyris, C. (1975). Dangers in applying results from experimental social psychology. *American Psychologist, 30*, 469-485.

Asch, S. (1955). Opinions and social pressure. *Scientific American, 193*, 31-35.

Atwell, J. E. (1981). Human rights in human subjects research. In A. J. Kimmel (Ed.), *Ethics of human subject research.* San Francisco: Jossey-Bass.

Ayer, A. J. (1963). *Philosophical essays.* London: Macmillan.

Babbage, C. (1969). *Reflections on the decline of science in England, and on some of its causes.* London: Gregg International (originally published in 1830).

Baratz, S. S. (1973). Applying the behavioral sciences to the needs of public policy making. *Professional Psychology, 4*, 216-223.

Baumrin, B. H. (1970). The immorality of irrelevance: The social role of science. In F. F. Korten, S. W. Cook, & J. I. Lacey (Eds.), *Psychology and the problems of society.* Washington, DC: APA.

Baumrind, D. (1964). Some thoughts on ethics of research: After reading Milgram's "Behavioral study of obedience." *American Psychologist, 19*, 421-423.

Baumrind, D. (1971). Principles of ethical conduct in the treatment of subjects: Reaction to the draft report of the Committee on Ethical Standards in Psychological Research. *American Psychologist, 26*, 887-896.

Baumrind, D. (1975). Metaethical and normative considerations governing the treatment of human subjects in the behavioral sciences. In E. C. Kennedy (Ed.), *Human rights and psychological research: A debate on psychology and ethics*. New York: Thomas Y. Crowell.

Baumrind, D. (1985). Research using intentional deception: Ethical issues revisited. *American Psychologist, 40*, 165-174.

Bazelon, D. L. (1982). Veils, values, and social responsibility. *American Psychologist, 37*, 115-121.

Beals, R. L. (1969). *Politics of social change*. Chicago: Aldine.

Beecher, H. K. (1966). Ethics and clinical research. *New England Journal of Medicine, 274*, 1354-1360.

Behavioral Sciences and the National Security. (1965). Report No. 4, and Part IX of the Hearings on *Winning the Cold War: The U.S. Ideological Offensive*, by the Subcommittee on International Organizations and Movements of the Committee on Foreign Affairs, House of Representatives. Washington, DC: Government Printing Office.

Bell, E. H., & Bronfenbrenner, U. (1959). Freedom and responsibility in research: Comments. *Human Organization, 18*, 49-52.

Bermant, G. et al. (1974). The logic of simulation in jury research. *Criminal Justice and Behavior, 1*, 224-233.

Bermant, G., Kelman, H. C., & Warwick, D. P. (1978). *The ethics of social intervention*. Washington, DC: Hemisphere.

Bermel, J. (1985). Prior publication: Two research studies, two views. *Hastings Center Report, 15*, 3-4.

Berscheid, E., Baron, R. S., Dermer, M., & Libman, M. (1973). Anticipating informed consent: An empirical approach. *American Psychologist, 28*, 913-925.

Bickman, L., & Zarantonello, M. (1978). The effects of deception and level of obedience on subjects' ratings of the Milgram study. *Personality and Social Psychology Bulletin, 4*, 81-85.

Bok, S., (1978). *Lying: Moral choice in public and private life*. New York: Pantheon.

Boruch, R. F. (1975). *Is a promise of confidentiality necessary? Sufficient? A review and a bibliography* (Research Rep. NIE-11/11X). Evanston, IL: Northwestern University, Evaluation Research Program.

Boruch, R. F., & Cecil, J. S. (1979). *Assuring the confidentiality of social research data*. Philadelphia: University of Pennsylvania Press.

Boruch, R. F., & Cecil, J. S. (1982). Statistical strategies for preserving privacy in direct inquiry. In J. E. Sieber (Ed.), *The ethics of social research: Surveys and experiments*. New York: Springer-Verlag.

Boruch, R. F., & Wothke, W. (Eds.). (1985). *Randomization and field experimentation*. San Francisco: Jossey-Bass.

Bower, R. T., & de Gasparis, P. (1978). *Ethics in social research: Protecting the interests of human subjects*. New York: Praeger.

Broad, C. D. (1930). *Five types of ethical theory*. London: Routledge & Kegan Paul.

Brock, T. C., & Becker, L. A. (1966). Debriefing and susceptibility to subsequent experimental manipulations. *Journal of Experimental Social Psychology, 2*, 314-323.

Brown, G. H., & Harding, F. D. (1973). *A comparison of methods of studying illicit drug usage* (HUMRO Tech. Rep. 75-14). Arlington, VA: Human Resources Research Organization.

Brown, P. G. (1975). Informed consent in social experimentation: Some cautionary notes. In A. M. Rivlin & P. M. Timpane (Eds.), *Ethical and legal issues of social experimentation*. Washington, DC: Brookings Institution.

Brymer, R. A., & Farris, B. (1967). Ethical and political dilemmas in the investigation of deviance: A study of juvenile delinquency. In G. Sjoberg (Ed.), *Ethics, politics, and social research*. Cambridge, MA: Shenkman.

Bunda, M. A. (1985). Alternative systems of ethics and their application to education and evaluation. *Evaluation and Program Planning, 8*, 25-36.

Campbell, D. T. (1969). Reforms as experiments. *American Psychologist, 24*, 409-429.

Campbell, D. T., Boruch, R. F., Schwartz, R. D., & Steinberg, J. (1977). Confidentiality-preserving modes of access to files and to interfile exchange for useful statistical analysis. *Evaluation Quarterly, 1*, 269-299.

Campbell, D. T., & Cecil, J. S. (1982). A proposed system of regulation for the protection of participants in low-risk areas of applied social research. In J. E. Sieber (Ed.), *The ethics of social research: Fieldwork, regulation and publication*. New York: Springer-Verlag.

Campbell, D. T., & Kimmel, A. J. (1985). *Guiding preventive intervention research centers for research validity* (Contract No. SSN 552-12-4531). Rockville, MD: Department of Health and Human Services.

Caplan, N., Morrison, A., & Stambaugh, R. J. (1975). *The use of social science knowledge in policy decisions at the national level*. Ann Arbor: University of Michigan, Institute for Social Research, Center for Research on Utilization of Scientific Knowledge.

Carroll, M. A., Schneider, H. G., & Wesley, G. R. (1985). *Ethics in the practice of psychology*. Englewood Cliffs, NJ: Prentice-Hall.

Caulfield, B. A. (1978). *The legal aspects of protective services for abused and neglected children*. Washington, DC: Government Printing Office.

Ceci, S. J., Peters, D., & Plotkin, J. (1985). Human subjects review, personal values, and the regulation of social science research. *American Psychologist, 40*, 994-1002.

Center for the Study of Ethics in the Professions. (1981). *Compilation of statements relating to standards of professional responsibility and freedom*. Chicago: Illinois Institute of Technology.

Chalk, R., Frankel, M. S., & Chafer, S. B. (1980). *AAAS Professional ethics activities in the scientific and engineering societies*. Washington, DC: American Association for the Advancement of Science.

Childress, J. (1975). The identification of ethical principles. In The National Commission for the Protection of Biomedical and Behavioral Research, *Appendix, Volume I: The Belmont Report*. Bethesda, MD: Department of Health, Education, and Welfare.

Clarke-Stewart, K. A. (1978). Popular primers for parents. *American Psychologist, 33*, 359-369.

Cohen, J. (1982). The cost of IRB reviews. In R. A. Greenwald, M. K. Ryan, J. E. Mulvihill (Eds.), *Human subjects research: A handbook for institutional review boards* (pp. 39-47). New York: Plenum.

Cole, J. R., & Cole, S. (1973). *Social stratification in science*. Chicago: University of Chicago Press.

Colgrove v. Battin, 413 U.S. 149 (1973).

Committee on Federal Agency Evaluation Research. (1975). *Protecting individual privacy in evaluation research*. Washington, DC: National Academy of Sciences.

Committee on National Statistics. (1979). *Privacy and confidentiality as factors in survey response.* Washington, DC: National Academy of Sciences.

Confrey, E. A. (1970). Should a government agency regulate ethical behavior? *Annals of the New York Academy of Sciences, 169,* 528-532.

Conner, R. F. (1982). Random assignment of clients in social experimentation. In J. E. Sieber (Ed.), *The ethics of social research: Surveys and experiments.* New York: Springer-Verlag.

Cook, S. W. (1970). Motives in a conceptual analysis of attitude related behavior. In W. J. Arnold & D. Levine (Eds.), *Nebraska symposium on motivation.* Lincoln: University of Nebraska Press.

Cook, T. D., & Campbell, D. T. (1979). *Quasi-experimentation: Design and analysis for field settings.* Boston: Houghton Mifflin.

Curran, W. J. (1969). Governmental regulation of the use of human subjects in medical research: The approach of two federal agencies. *Daedalus, 98*(2), 542-594.

Dalglish, T. (1976). *Protecting human subjects in social and behavioral research: Ethics, law and the DHEW rules: A critique.* Berkeley: University of California, Berkeley, Center for Research in Management Science.

Department of Health, Education and Welfare. (1974, May 30). Protection of human subjects. *Federal Register, 39,* 18914-18920.

Department of Health, Education, and Welfare. (1978). Protection of human subjects; institutional review board; report and recommendations of National Commission for the Protection of Human Subjects of Biomedical and Behavioral Research. *Federal Register, 43,* 56174-56198.

Diener, E., & Crandall, R. (1978). *Ethics in social and behavioral research.* Chicago: University of Chicago Press.

Dill, C. A., Gilden, E. R., Hill, P. C., & Hanselka, L. L. (1982). Federal human subjects regulations: A methodological artifact? *Personality and Social Psychology Bulletin, 8,* 417-425.

Dillehay, R. C., & Nietzel, M. T. (1980). Constructing a science of jury behavior. In L. Wheeler, (Ed.), *Review of personality and social psychology.* Beverly Hills, CA: Sage.

Doob, A. N. (1983). The reliability of ethical reviews: Is it desirable? *Canadian Psychologist, 24,* 269-270.

Douglas, M., & Wildavksy, A. (1982). *Risk and culture.* Berkeley: University of California Press.

Eaton, W. O. (1983). The reliability of ethical reviews: Some initial empirical findings. *Canadian Psychologist, 24,* 14-18.

Eckler, A. R. (1972). *The Bureau of the Census.* New York: Praeger.

Edsall, G. A. (1969). A positive approach to the problem of human experimentation. *Daedalus, 98,* 463-478.

Epstein, Y. M., Suedfeld, P., & Silverstein, S. J. (1973). Subjects' expectations and reactions to some behaviors of experimenters. *American Psychologist, 28,* 212-221.

Esposito, J. L., Agard, E., & Rosnow, R. L. (1984). Can confidentiality of data pay off? *Personality and Individual Differences, 5,* 477-480.

Evaluation Research Society Standards Committee. (1982). Evaluation Research Society standards for program evaluation. *New Directions for Program Evaluation, 15,* 7-19.

Faden, R. R., & Beauchamp, T. L. (1986). *A history and theory of informed consent.* New York: Oxford University Press.

Feige, E. L., & Watts, H. W. (1970). Protection of privacy through microaggregation. In R. L. Bisco (Ed.), *Data bases, computers, and the social scientist.* New York: Wiley-Interscience.

Fersch, E. A., Jr. (1980). Ethical issues for psychologists in court settings. In J. Monahan (Ed.), *Who is the client? The ethics of intervention in the criminal justice system.* Washington, DC: American Psychological Association.

Fischer, F. (1980). *Politics, values, and public policy: The problem of methodology.* Boulder, CO: Westview.

Fisher, K. (1982, November). The spreading stain of fraud. *APA Monitor,* pp. 7-8.

Fisher, K. (1986, May). Ethics in research: Having respect for the subject. *APA Monitor, 17*(5), 1, 34.

Fo, W. S., & O'Donnell, C. R. (1975). The buddy system: Effects of community intervention on delinquent offenses. *Behavior Therapy, 6,* 522-524.

Folsom, R. E. (1974). *A randomized response validation study: Comparison of direct and randomized reporting of DUI arrests* (Final Report, 2550-807). Chapel Hill, NC: Research Triangle Institute.

Forsyth, D. R. (1980). A taxonomy of ethical ideologies. *Journal of Personality and Social Psychology, 39,* 175-184.

Fowler, F. J., Jr. (1984). *Survey research methods.* Beverly Hills, CA: Sage.

Fox, J. A., & Tracy, P. E. (1984). Measuring associations with randomized response. *Social Science Research, 13*(2), 188-197.

Francis, H.W.S. (1982). Of gossips, eavesdroppers, and peeping toms. *Journal of Medical Ethics, 8,* 134-143.

Frankel, M. S. (1975). The development of policy guidelines governing human experimentation in the United States. *Ethics in Science and Medicine, 2,* 43-59.

Frankena, W. K. (1973). *Ethics* (2nd ed.). Englewood Cliffs, NJ: Prentice-Hall.

Frankena, W. K., & Granrose, J. T. (Eds.). (1974). *Introductory readings in ethics.* Englewood Cliffs, NJ: Prentice-Hall.

Freedman, M. H. (1975). *Lawyers' ethics in an adversary system.* Indianapolis, IN: Bobbs-Merrill.

Gardner, G. T. (1978). Effects of federal human subjects regulations on data obtained in environmental stressor research. *Journal of Personality and Social Psychology, 36,* 628-634.

Garner, R. T., & Rosen, B. (1967). *Moral philosophy: A systematic introduction to normative ethics and meta-ethics.* New York: Macmillian.

Georgoudi, M., & Rosnow, R. L. (1985). Notes toward a contextualist understanding of social psychology. *Personality and Social Psychology Bulletin, 11,* 5-22.

Gergen, K. J. (1973). Social psychology as history. *Journal of Personality and Social Psychology, 26,* 309-320.

Gersten, J. C., Langner, T. S., & Simcha-Fagan, O. (1979). Developmental patterns of types of behavioral disturbance and secondary prevention. *International Journal of Mental Health, 7,* 132-149.

Giddens, A. (1976). *New rules of sociological method.* London: Hutchinson.

Giddens, A. (1979). *Central problems in social theory.* London: Macmillan.

Glazer, M. (1972). *The research adventure.* New York: Random House.

Glynn, K. (1978). *Regulations regarding the use of human subjects in research: Effects on investigator's ethical sensitivity, research practices, and research priorities.* Paper presented at the annual meeting of the American Sociological Association, San Francisco, CA.

Golann, S. E. (1970). Ethical standards for psychology: Development and revision, 1938-1968. *Annals of the New York Academy of Sciences, 169,* 398-405.

Goldman, J., & Katz, M. D. (1982). Inconsistency and institutional review boards. *Journal of the American Medical Association, 248,* 197-202.

Gove, W. R. (1980). *The labeling of deviance* (2nd ed.). Beverly Hills, CA: Sage.

Gove, W. R. (Ed.). (1982). *Deviance and mental illness.* Beverly Hills, CA: Sage.

Granville, A. C., Johnston, J., & Nolan, N. K. (1983). *Using television to promote adolescent mental health. Search for a mandate* (Vol. 3). Ann Arbor: University of Michigan, Institute for Social Research.

Greenberg, B. G., Horvitz, D. G., & Abernathy, J. R. (1974). A comparison of randomized response designs. In F. Proschan & R. J. Serfling (Eds.), *Reliability and biometry.* Philadelphia: SIAM.

Gueron, J. M. (1985). The demonstration of state work/welfare initiatives. In R. F. Boruch & W. Wothke (Eds.), *Randomization and field experimentation.* San Francisco: Jossey-Bass.

Hamsher, J. H., & Reznikoff, M. (1967). Ethical standards in psychological research and graduate training: A study of attitudes within the profession. *Proceedings, 75th Annual Convention, American Psychological Association, 2,* 203-204.

Holden, C. (1979). Ethics in social science research. *Science, 206,* 537-540.

Holder, A. R. (1982). Do researchers and subjects have a fiduciary relationship? *IRB: A Review of Human Subjects Research 4,* 6-7.

Holton, G. (1973). *Thematic origins of scientific thought: Keplar to Einstein.* Cambridge, MA: Harvard University Press.

Horowitz, I. L. (1967). *The rise and fall of Project Camelot.* Cambridge: MIT Press.

Humphreys, L. (1970). *Tearoom trade.* Chicago: Aldine.

Institute for Social Research. (1976). *Research involving human subjects.* Ann Arbor: University of Michigan.

Jaffe, L. L. (1969). Law as a system of control. *Daedalus, 98,* 406-426.

Jason, L. A., & Bogat, G. A. (1983). Preventive behavioral interventions. In R. D. Felner, L. A. Jason, J. N. Moritsugu, & S. S. Farber (Eds.), *Preventive psychology: Theory, research and practice.* Elmsford, NY: Pergamon.

Jerrell, S. L., & Jerrell, J. M. (1985). Road signs in ethical quicksand. *Evaluation and Program Planning, 8,* 73-76.

Johnson, C. G. (1982). Risks in the publication of fieldwork. In J. E. Sieber (Ed.), *The ethics of social research: Fieldwork, regulation, and publication.* New York: Springer-Verlag.

Johnson, P. L. (1985). Ethical dilemmas in evaluating programs with family court related clients. *Evaluation and Program Planning, 8,* 45-51.

Johnston, J., Blumenfeld, P., & Isler, L. (1983). *Using television to promote adolescent mental health. Process and effects in classroom settings* (Vol. 2). Ann Arbor: University of Michigan, Institute for Social Research.

Joint Committee on Standards for Educational Evaluation. (1981). *Standards for evaluations of educational programs, projects, and materials.* New York: McGraw-Hill.

Jones, J. H. (1981). *Bad blood.* New York: Free Press.

Kant, I. (1965). *The metaphysical elements of justice.* Indianapolis: Bobbs-Merrill (originally published in 1797).

Katz, J. (1972). *Experimentation with human beings.* New York: Russell Sage.

Kelman, H. C. (1965). Manipulation of human behavior: An ethical dilemma for the social scientist. *Journal of Social Issues, 21,* 31-46.

Kelman, H. C. (1967). Human use of human subjects: The problem of deception in social psychological experiments. *Psychological Bulletin, 67,* 1-11.

Kelman, H. C. (1968). *A time to speak: On human values and social research.* San Francisco: Jossey-Bass.

Kelman, H. C. (1972). The rights of the subject in social research: An analysis in terms of relative power and legitimacy. *American Psychologist, 27,* 989-1016.

Kelman, H. C., & Warwick, D. P. (1978). The ethics of social intervention: Goals, means, and consequences. In G. Bermant, H. C. Kelman, & D. P. Warwick (Eds.), *The ethics of social intervention*. Washington, DC: Hemisphere.

Kershaw, D. N. (1975). The New Jersey negative income tax experiment. In G. M. Lyons (Ed.), *Social research and public policies*. Hanover, NH: Dartmouth College Public Affairs Center.

Kidder, L. H., & Judd, C. M. (1986). *Selltiz, Wrightsman and Cook's research methods in social relations* (5th ed.). New York: Holt, Rinehart & Winston.

Kiesler, C. A. (1980). Mental health policy as a field of inquiry for psychology. *American Psychologist, 35*, 1066-1080.

Kimmel, A. J. (1983). Predicting the conclusions of risk-benefit assessments in psychology from characteristics of the evaluator. *Dissertation Abstracts International, 44*, 360.

Kimmel, A. J. (1985a). *Ethical issues in prevention research*. Unpublished manuscript.

Kimmel, A. J. (1985b, March). *The ethics of gossip: The right to know versus the right to privacy*. Paper presented at the Eastern Psychological Association, Boston.

King, F. W. (1970). Anonymous versus identifiable questionnaires in drug usage surveys. *American Psychologist, 25*, 982-985.

Knerr, C. R., Jr. (1982). What to do before and after a subpoena of data arrives. In J. E. Sieber (Ed.), *The ethics of social research: Surveys and experiments*. New York: Springer-Verlag.

Koch, S. (1981). The nature and limits of psychological knowledge: Lessons of a century qua "science." *American Psychologist, 36*, 257-269.

Kramer, J. R. (1967). Resistance to sociological data: A case study. In P. F. Lazarsfeld, W. H. Sewell, & H. L. Wilensky (Eds.), *The uses of sociology*. New York: Basic Books.

Krasner, L., & Houts, A. C. (1984). A study of the "value" systems of behavioral scientists. *American Psychologist, 39*, 840-850.

Krotki, K., & Fox, B. (1974). The randomized response technique, the interview, and the self administered questionnaire: An empirical comparison of fertility reports. *Proceedings of the American Statistical Association: Social statistics section* (pp. 367-371). Washington, DC: ASA.

Ladimer, I. (1970). Protecting participants in human studies. *Annals of the New York Academy of Sciences, 169*, 564-572.

Lamberth, J., & Kimmel, A. J. (1981). Ethical issues and responsibilities in applying scientific behavioral knowledge. In A. J. Kimmel (Ed.), *Ethics of human subject research*. San Francisco: Jossey-Bass.

Lerner, D., & Lasswell, H. D. (1951). *The policy sciences*. Stanford, CA: Stanford University Press.

Lasswell, H. D. (1951). *The political writings of Harold D. Lasswell*. Glencoe: Free Press.

Levin, J. (1981). Ethical problems in sociological research. In A. J. Kimmel (Ed.), *Ethics of human subject research*. San Francisco: Jossey-Bass.

Levine, R. J. (1975a). The nature and definition of informed consent in various research settings. In the National Commission for the Protection of Biomedical and Behavioral Research, *Appendix, Volume I: The Belmont Report*. Bethesda, MD: Department of Health, Education, and Welfare.

Levine, R. J. (1975b). The role of assessment of risk-benefit criteria in the determination of the appropriateness of research involving human subjects. In the National Commission for the Protection of Biomedical and Behavioral Research, *Appendix, Volume I: The Belmont Report*. Bethesda, MD: Department of Health, Education, and Welfare.

Lewin, K. (1947). Group decision and social change. In T. M. Newcomb & E. L. Hartley (Eds.), *Readings in social psychology*. New York: Holt.

Lindblom, C. E., & Cohen, D. (1979). *Usable knowledge: Social science and social problem solving.* New Haven, CT: Yale University Press.

Liu, P. T., Chow, L. P., & Mosley, W. H. (1975). Use of the randomized response technique with a new randomizing technique. *Journal of the American Statistical Association, 70,* 324-332.

Loftus, E. F., & Fries, J. F. (1979). Informed consent may be hazardous to health. *Science. 204,* 11.

London, M., & Bray, D. W. (1980). Ethical issues in testing and evaluation for personnel decisions. *American Psychologist, 35,* 890-901.

Loo, C. M. (1982). Vulnerable populations: Case studies in crowding research. In J. E. Sieber (Ed.), *The ethics of social research: Surveys and experiments.* New York: Springer-Verlag.

Lorion, R. P. (1983). Evaluating preventive interventions: Guidelines for the serious social change agent. In R. D. Felner, L. A. Jason, J. N. Moritsugu, & S. S. Farber (Eds.), *Preventive psychology: Theory, research and practice.* Elmsford, NY: Pergamon.

Lorion, R. P. (1984). Research issues in the design and evaluation of preventive interventions. In J. P. Bowker (Ed.), *Education for primary prevention in social work.* New York: Council on Social Work Education.

Lowman, R. P., & Soule, L. M. (1981). Professional ethics and the use of humans in research. In A. J. Kimmel (Ed.), *Ethics of human subject research.* San Francisco: Jossey-Bass.

Lueptow, L., Mueller, S. A., Hammes, R. R., & Master, L. S. (1977). The impact of informed consent regulations on response rate and response bias. *Sociological Methods and Research, 6,* 183-204.

Luria, S. E. (1976). Biological aspects of ethical principles. *Journal of Medicine and Philosophy, 1,* 332-336.

Lynn, L. E., Jr. (1977). Policy relevant social research: What does it look like? In M. Guttentag & S. Saar (Eds.), *Evaluation studies review annual* (Vol. 2). Beverly Hills, CA: Sage.

Macklin, R., & Sherwin, S. (1975). Experimenting on human subjects: Philosophical perspectives. *Case Western Reserve Law Review, 25,* 434-471.

Mahoney, M. J. (1976). *Scientist as subject: The psychological imperative.* Cambridge, MA: Ballinger.

McCarthy, C. R. (1981). The development of federal regulations for social research. In A. J. Kimmel (Ed.), *Ethics of human subject research.* San Francisco: Jossey-Bass.

McCord, J. (1978). A thirty-year follow-up of treatment effects. *American Psychologist, 33,* 284-289.

McGuire, W. (1965). Discussion of William N. Schoenfeld's paper. In O. Klineberg & R. Christie (Eds.), *Perspectives in social psychology.* New York: Holt, Rinehart & Winston.

Meehl, P. (1971). Law and the fireside inductions: Some reflections of a clinical psychologist. *Journal of Social Issues, 27,* 65-100.

Merton, R. K. (1973). *The sociology of science: Theoretical and empirical investigations.* Chicago: University of Chicago Press.

Milgram, S. (1963). Behavioral study of obedience. *Journal of Abnormal and Social Psychology, 67,* 371-378.

Milgram, S. (1964). Issues in the study of obedience: A reply to Baumrind. *American Psychologist, 19,* 848-852.

Milgram, S. (1965). Some conditions of obedience and disobedience to authority. *Human Relations, 18,* 57-76.

Milgram, S. (1974). *Obedience to authority*. New York: Harper & Row.

Mill, J. S. (1957). *Utilitarianism*. New York: Bobbs-Merrill (originally published in 1861).

Miller, A. (1972). Role playing: An alternative to deception? *American Psychologist, 27*, 623-636.

Miller, G. A. (1969). Psychology as a means of promoting human welfare. *American Psychologist, 24*, 1063-1075.

Miller, R., & Willner, H. S. (1974). The two-part consent form: A suggestion for promoting free and informed consent. *New England Journal of Medicine, 290*, 964-966.

Mills, J. (1976). A procedure for explaining experiments involving deception. *Personality and Social Psychology Bulletin, 2*, 3-13.

Mirvis, P. H., & Seashore, S. E. (1982). Creating ethical relationships in organizational research. In J. E. Sieber (Ed.), *The ethics of social research: Surveys and experiments*. New York: Springer-Verlag.

Mitroff, I. I. (1974). *The subjective side of science*. New York: Elsevier.

Monahan, J. (Ed.). (1980). *Who is the client? The ethics of intervention in the criminal justice system*. Washington, DC: American Psychological Association.

Moore, F. D. (1970). Therapeutic innovation: Ethical boundaries in the initial clinical trials of new drugs and surgical procedures. In P. A. Freund (Ed.), *Experimentation with human subjects*. New York: George Braziller.

Muchinsky, P. M. (1983). *Psychology applied to work*. Homewood, IL: Dorsey.

Muñoz, R. F. (1983, May 15-17). *Prevention intervention research: A sample of ethical dilemmas*. Paper presented at the NIMH State-of-the-Art Workshop on "Ethics and Primary Prevention," California State University, Northridge.

Muñoz, R. F., Glish, M., Soo-Hoo, T., & Robertson, J. (1982). The San Francisco mood survey project: Preliminary work toward the prevention of depression. *American Journal of Community Psychology, 10*, 317-329.

Murray, T. H. (1980). Learning to deceive. *Hastings Center Report, 10*(2), 11-13.

Natanson, M. (1975). A philosophical perspective on the assessment of risk-benefit criteria in connection with research involving human subjects. In The National Commission for the Protection of Biomedical and Behavioral Research, *Appendix, Volume II: The Belmont Report*. Bethesda, MD: Department of Health, Education, and Welfare.

National Center on Child Abuse and Neglect. (1978). *Child abuse and neglect: State reporting laws*. Washington, DC: Government Printing Office.

Nejelski, P. (Ed.). (1976). *Social research in conflict with law and ethics*. Cambridge, MA: Ballinger.

Nemeth, C. (1981). Jury trials: Psychology and law. In L. Berkowitz (Ed.), *Advances in experimental social psychology* (Vol. 13). New York: Academic Press.

O'Donnell, J. M. (1979). The crisis of experimentalism in the 1920s: E. G. Boring and his uses of history. *American Psychologist, 34*, 289-295.

Orlans, H. (1973). *Contracting for knowledge*. San Francisco: Jossey-Bass.

Orne, M. T. (1962). On the social psychology of the psychological experiment: With particular reference to demand characteristics and their implications. *American Psychologist, 17*, 776-783.

Pahel, K., & Schiller, M. (Eds.). (1970). *Readings in contemporary ethical theory*. Englewood Cliffs, NJ: Prentice-Hall.

Panel on Privacy and Behavioral Research. (1967). Privacy and behavioral research: Preliminary summary of the report of the Panel on Privacy and Behavioral Research. *Science, 155*, 535-538.

Pappworth, M. H. (1967). *Human guinea pigs: Experimentation on man.* Boston: Beacon.

Pattullo, E. L. (1980). Who risks what in social research? *Hastings Center Report, 10,* 15-18.

Pepitone, A. (1981). Lessons from the history of social psychology. *American Psychologist, 36,* 972-985.

Pervin, L. A. (1978). *Current controversies and issues in personality.* New York: John Wiley.

Pfeiffer, J. W., & Jones, J. E. (1977). Ethical considerations in consulting. In J. E. Jones & J. W. Pfeiffer (Eds.), *The 1977 annual for group facilitators.* La Jolla, CA: University Associates.

Polanyi, M. (1958). *Personal knowledge: Towards a post-critical philosophy.* New York: Harper & Row.

Polanyi, M. (1966). A society of explorers. In *The tacit dimension* (Chap. 3). Garden City: Doubleday.

Polanyi, M. (1969). *Knowing and being.* London: Routledge & Kegan Paul.

Polich, J. M., Ellickson, P. L., Reuter, P., & Kahan, J. P. (1984). *Strategies for controlling adolescent drug use.* Santa Monica, CA: Rand.

Powers, E., & Witmer, H. (1951). *An experiment in the prevention of delinquency: The Cambridge-Somerville youth study.* New York: Columbia University Press.

Rainwater, L., & Yancey, W. (1967). *The Moynihan Report and the politics of controversy.* Cambridge: MIT Press.

Ravetz, J. R. (1971). *Scientific knowledge and its social problems.* Oxford: Clarendon.

Rawls, J. (1971). *A theory of justice.* Cambridge, MA: Harvard University Press.

Reaser, J. M., Hartsock, S., & Hoehn, A. J. (1975). *A test of the forced alternative random response questionnaire technique* (HUMRO Tech. Rep. 75-9). Arlington, VA: Human Resources Research Organization.

Redlich, F., & Mollica, R. F. (1976). Overview: Ethical issues in contemporary psychiatry. *American Journal of Psychiatry, 133,* 125-136.

Reese, H. W., & Fremouw, W. J. (1984). Normal and normative ethics in behavioral sciences. *American Psychologist, 39,* 863-876.

Rein, M. (1976). *Social science and public policy.* New York: Penguin.

Resnick, J. H., & Schwartz, T. (1973). Ethical standards as an independent variable in psychological research. *American Psychologist, 28,* 134-139.

Reynolds, P. D. (1972). On the protection of human subjects and social science. *International Social Science Journal, 24,* 693-719.

Reynolds, P. D. (1979). *Ethical dilemmas and social science research.* San Francisco: Jossey-Bass.

Riecken, H. W., & Boruch, R. F. (Eds.). (1974). *Social experimentation: A method for planning and evaluating social intervention.* New York: Academic Press.

Rivlin, A. M., & Timpane, P. M. (Eds.). (1975). *Ethical and legal issues of social experimentation.* Washington, DC: Brookings Institution.

Robinson, R., & Greenberg, C. I. (1980, September). Informed consent: An artifact in human crowding. In J. R. Aiello (Chair), *Crowding and high population density.* Symposium presented at the meeting of the American Psychological Association, Montreal.

Roe, A. (1961). The psychology of the scientist. *Science, 134,* 456-459.

Rosenthal, R., & Rosnow, R. L. (Eds.). (1969). *Artifact in behavioral research.* New York: Academic Press.

Rosenthal, R., & Rosnow, R. L. (1975). *The volunteer subject.* New York: John Wiley.

Rosenthal, R., & Rosnow, R. L. (1984). Applying Hamlet's question to the ethical conduct of research: A conceptual addendum. *American Psychologist, 39,* 561-563.

Rosnow, R. L. (1981). *Paradigms in transition: The methodology of social inquiry.* New York: Oxford University Press.

Ross, W. D. (1930). *The right and the good.* Oxford: Clarendon.

Ruebhausen, O. M., & Brim, O. G., Jr. (1966). Privacy and behavioral research. *American Psychologist, 21,* 423-437.

Rugg, E. A. (1975). Ethical judgments of social research involving experimental deception. *Dissertation Abstracts International, 36,* 4-B.

Sahakian, W. S. (1974). *Ethics: An introduction to theories and problems.* New York: Barnes & Noble.

Saks, M. J. (1976). The limits of scientific jury selection: Ethical and empirical. *Jurimetrics Journal, 17,* 3-22.

Sarason, S. B. (1978). The nature of problem solving in social action. *American Psychologist, 33,* 370-380.

Sarason, S. B. (1981). *Psychology misdirected.* New York: Free Press.

Schelling, T. C. (1975). General comments. In A. M. Rivlin & P. M. Timpane (Eds.), *Ethical and legal issues of social experimentation.* Washington, DC: Brookings Institution.

Schlenker, B. R., & Forsyth, D. R. (1977). On the ethics of psychological research. *Journal of Experimental Social Psychology, 13,* 369-396.

Schuler, H. (1982). *Ethical problems in psychological research.* New York: Academic Press.

Sheinfeld, S. N., & Lord, G. L. (1981). The ethics of evaluation researchers. *Evaluation Review, 5,* 377-391.

Sieber, J. E. (1980). Being ethical: Professional and personal decisions in program evaluation. *New Directions for Program Evaluation, 7,* 51-61.

Sieber, J. E. (Ed.). (1982a). *The ethics of social research: Surveys and experiments.* New York: Springer-Verlag.

Sieber, J. E. (1982b). Ethical dilemmas in social research. In J. E. Sieber (Ed.), *The ethics of social research: Surveys and experiments.* New York: Springer-Verlag.

Sieber, J. E. (1983). Deception in social research III: The nature and limits of debriefing. *IRB: A Review of Human Subjects Research, 5,* 1-4.

Sieber, J. E., & Stanley, B. (1988). Ethical and professional dimensions of socially sensitive research. *American Psychologist, 43,* 49-55.

Seiler, L. H., & Murtha, J. M. (1981). Final regulations for the protection of human subjects of research provide a balanced compromise. *Society for the Advancement of Social Psychology Newsletter, 7,* 6-7.

Singer, E. (1978). Informed consent: Consequences for response rate and response quality in social surveys. *American Sociological Review, 43,* 144-162.

Singer, E., & Frankel, M. R. (1982). Informed consent procedures in telephone interviews. *American Sociological Review, 47,* 416-427.

Sjoberg, G. (1967). Project Camelot: Selected reactions and personal reflections. In G. Sjoberg (Ed.), *Ethics, politics, and social research.* Cambridge, MA: Schenkman.

Smith, A., & Berard, S. P. (1982). Why are human subjects less concerned about ethically problematic research than human subjects committees? *Journal of Applied Social Psychology, 12,* 209-221.

Smith, D. H. (1978). Scientific knowledge and forbidden truths—are there things we should not know? *Hastings Center Report, 8,* 30-35.

Smith, N. L. (1985a). Introduction: Moral and ethical problems in evaluation. *Evaluation and Program Planning, 8,* 1-3.

Smith, N. L. (1985b). Some characteristics of moral problems in evaluation practice. *Evaluation and Program Planning, 8,* 5-11.

Society for Industrial and Organizational Psychology, Inc. (1987). *Principles for the validation and use of personnel selection procedures* (3rd ed.). College Park, MD: Author.

Sommer, R., & Sommer, B. A. (1983). Mystery in Milwaukee: Early intervention, IQ, and psychology textbooks. *American Psychologist, 38,* 982-985.

Spivack, G., Platt, J. J., & Shure, M. B. (1976). *The problem-solving approach to adjustment.* San Francisco: Jossey-Bass.

Spivack, G., & Shure, M. B. (1974). *Social adjustment of young children: A cognitive approach to solving real-life problems.* San Francisco: Jossey-Bass.

Steininger, M., Newell, J. D., & Garcia, L. T. (1984). *Ethical issues in psychology.* Homewood, IL: Dorsey.

Stricker, L. J., Messick, S., & Jackson, D. M. (1967). Suspicion of deception: Implications for conformity research. *Journal of Personality and Social Psychology, 5,* 379-389.

Sullivan, D. S., & Deiker, T. E. (1973). Subject-experimenter perceptions of ethical issues in human research. *American Psychologist, 28,* 587-591.

Tanke, E. D., & Tanke, T. J. (1982). Regulation and education: The role of the institutional review board in social science research. In J. E. Sieber (Ed.), *The ethics of social research: Fieldwork, regulation, and publication.* New York: Springer-Verlag.

Tarasoff v. Regents of the University of California. (1976). *California Reporter, 131,* 14.

Tedeschi, J. T., & Rosenfeld, P. (1981). The experimental research controversy at SUNY: A case study. In A. J. Kimmel (Ed.), *Ethics of human subject research.* San Francisco: Jossey-Bass.

Titus, H. H., & Keeton, M. (1973). *Ethics for today* (5th ed.). New York: D. Van Nostrand.

Tracy, P. E., & Fox, J. A. (1981). The validity of randomized responses for sensitive measurements. *American Sociological Review, 46,* 187-200.

Trochim, W. (1982). *Research design for program evaluation: The regression-discontinuity approach.* Beverly Hills, CA: Sage.

Vaughan, T. R. (1967). Governmental intervention in social research: Political and ethical dimensions in the Wichita jury recordings. In G. Sjoberg (Ed.), *Ethics, politics, and social research.* Cambridge, MA: Schenkman.

Veatch, R. M., & Sollitto, S. (1973). Human experimentation: The ethical questions persist. *Hastings Center Report, 3*(3), 1-3.

Vidich, A. J., & Bensman, J. (1958). *Small town in mass society: Class, power, and religion in a rural community.* Princeton, NJ: Princeton University Press.

Vidmar, N. (1979). The other issues in jury simulation research. *Law and Human Behavior, 3,* 95-106.

Walton, R. E. (1978). Ethical issues in the practice of organization development. In G. Bermant, H. C. Kelman, & D. P. Warwick (Eds.), *The ethics of social intervention.* Washington, DC: Hemisphere.

Warner, S. L. (1965). Randomized response: A survey technique for eliminating evasive answer bias. *Journal of the American Statistical Association, 60,* 63-69.

Warner, S. L. (1971). The linear randomized responsive model. *Journal of the American Statistical Association, 66,* 884-888.

Warwick, D. P., & Kelman, H. C. (1973). Ethical issues in social intervention. In G. Zaltman (Ed.), *Processes and phenomena of social change.* New York: John Wiley.

Watkins, B., Perloff, L. S., Wortman, C. B., & Johnston, J. (1983). *Using television to promote adolescent mental health: Mental health messages on prime-time television* (Vol. 1). Ann Arbor: University of Michigan, Institute for Social Research.

Weber, M. (1949). *The methodology of the social sciences* (Trans. and eds. E. A. Shils & H. A. Finch). New York: Free Press.

Weiss, C. H. (1978). Improving the linkage between social research and public policy. In L. E. Lynn (Ed.), *Knowledge and policy: The uncertain condition.* Washington, DC: National Academy of Sciences.

Welt, L. G. (1961). Reflections on the problems of human experimentation. *Connecticut Medicine, 25*, 75-79.

West, S. G., Gunn, S. P., & Chernicky, P. (1975). Ubiquitous Watergate: An attributional analysis. *Journal of Personality and Social Psychology, 32*, 55-65.

West, S. G., & Gunn, S. P. (1978). Some issues of ethics and social psychology. *American Psychologist, 33*, 30-38.

Westin, A. F. (1968). *Privacy and freedom.* New York: Atheneum.

Wildavsky, A. (1979). *Speaking truth to power: The art and craft of policy analysis.* Boston: Little, Brown.

Wolfgang, M. E. (1981). Confidentiality in criminological research and other ethical issues. *Journal of Criminal Law and Criminology, 72*, 345-361.

Wortman, C. B., & Rabinovitz, V. C. (1979). Randomization: The fairest of them all. In L. Sechrest et al. (Eds.), *Evaluation studies review annual* (Vol. 4). Beverly Hills, CA: Sage.

Zdep, S. M., & Rhodes, I. N. (1977). Making the randomized response technique work. *Public Opinion Quarterly, 41*, 531-537.

Zeisel, H. (1970). Reducing the hazards of human experiments through modifications in research design. *Annals of the New York Academy of Sciences, 169*, 475-486.

# SUBJECT INDEX

# ABOUT THE AUTHOR

Allan J. Kimmel is Assistant Professor of Behavioral Science at Fitchburg State College, where he teaches courses in social psychology and industrial/organizational psychology. He previously taught at Moravian College, where he also directed a certificate program in human resources administration. He received his Ph.D. in social psychology from Temple University in 1983. His doctoral dissertation focused on predictable biases that underlie the ethical decision making of professional American psychologists. When he was a graduate student, his interests in ethics involved issues pertaining to laboratory research with human subjects and he edited a book on the topic. Since that time his attention has turned to the broader ethical concerns that emerge in applied settings. Dr. Kimmel is a member of the Society for the Psychological Study of Social Issues, a past associate member of the Hastings Center Institute of Society, Ethics, and the Life Sciences, and serves on the steering committee for the Society for the Advancement of Social Psychology. In addition to his work on research ethics, he has published articles on the social psychology of hearsay.